W9-BZT-295

CULTURES OF THE WORLD
Libya

mc Marshall Cavendish
Benchmark
New York

PICTURE CREDITS

Cover: © Gary Cook/Alamy
Ahmed Masri/AFP/Getty Images: 110 • Alexis Duclos/Gamma-Rapho/Getty Images: 50 • Amerens Hedwich/
Lonely Planet Images: 10, 114 • Anthony Ham/Lonely Planet Images: 16, 36, 84, 102, 122, 128 • Behrouz Mehri/
AFP/Getty Images: 57 • Carl de Souza/AFP/Getty Images: 90 • Doug McKinlay/Lonely Planet Images: 22, 29,
45, 64, 100 • Edoardo Fornaciari/Gamma-Rapho/Getty Images: 49 • Frans Lemmens/Lonely Planet Images: 3,
14, 68, 92, 127 • Getty images: 1, 18, 58, 60, 62, 86, 94, 96, 104, 106, 124, 126 • Gianluigi Guercia/AFP/Getty
Images: 120 • Inmagine: 13, 20, 55, 65, 67, 70, 73, 74, 75, 76, 79, 83, 103 • James L. Stanfield/Geographic Stock:
77, 82, 111 • Jane Sweeney/Lonely Planet Images: 56, 123 • Joseph Eid/AFP/Getty Images: 44 • Mahmud Turkia/
AFP/Getty Images: 6, 42, 47, 116, 119 • Marco Longari/AFP/Getty Images: 7 • Mario Tama/Getty Images: 38
• Mary Beth Sheridan/The Washington Post/Getty Images: 80 • Michel Ginfray/GAMMA/Gamma-Rapho/Getty
Images: 31 • Patrick Syder/Lonely Planet Images: 25, 54, 105, 108 • Philippe Desmazes/AFP/Getty Images: 8
• Seyllou/AFP/Getty Images: 40 • Tony Wheeler/Lonely Planet Images: 5, 66

PRECEDING PAGE

Two Libyan boys pose for the camera in Old Medina.

Publisher (U.S.): Michelle Bisson
Writers: Peter Malcolm, Elie Loslenben, Yong Jui Lin
Editors: Deborah Grahame-Smith, Stephanie Pee
Copyreader: Tara Tomczyk
Designers: Nancy Sabato, Bernard Go
Cover picture researcher: Tracey Engel
Picture researcher: Joshua Ang

Marshall Cavendish Benchmark
99 White Plains Road
Tarrytown, NY 10591
Website: www.marshallcavendish.us

Library of Congress Cataloging-in-Publication Data
Malcolm, Peter, 1937-
 Libya / Peter Malcolm, Elie Loslenben, Yong Jui Lin.
   p. cm. -- (Cultures of the world)
 Summary: "Provides comprehensive information on the geography, history, wildlife, governmental structure,
economy, cultural diversity, peoples, religion, and culture of Libya"--Provided by publisher.
 Includes bibliographical references and index.
 ISBN 978-1-60870-992-2 (print)
 ISBN: 978-1-60870-999-1 (ebook)
 1. Libya—Juvenile literature. I. Loslenben, Elie. II. Yong, Jui Lin. III. Title. IV. Series: Cultures of the world
(3rd ed.)

DT215.M3 2013
961.2—dc23   2011042593

Printed in Malaysia
7 6 5 4 3 2 1

CONTENTS

LIBYA TODAY

WITH THE DEATH OF COLONEL GADDAFI ON OCTOBER 20, 2011, the bloody Libyan civil war came to an end. The dictator was found hiding in a sewage pipe, and begged for mercy from resistance fighters. He was eventually shot. Libyans all around the world rejoiced at the death of the mercurial leader who had ruled over their oil-rich country for 42 years. The chairman of the National Transitional Council executive board, Mahmoud Jibril, said that elections should be held within a period of eight months. Libya is currently producing 300,000 barrels of oil a day, a welcome change from zero barrels during the depths of the war. The country should be back at its prewar output of 1.6 million barrels of oil per day within 15 months, according to Jibril.

The situation began on February 15, 2011, with peaceful protests that were met with military force by the Gaddafi regime. After the February 15 uprising, as the rebels appeared to be outgunned and outnumbered, the United Nations (UN) Security Council voted to authorize military action, a risky foreign intervention aimed at averting a bloody rout of the rebels by loyalist forces. On March 19, American and European forces began a broad campaign of strikes against Gaddafi

Oil and gas plants in Libya. The petroleum industry generates a large proportion of the country's revenue.

and his government, unleashing warplanes and missiles in a military intervention on a scale not seen in the Arab world since the start of the Iraq War. By late May, weeks of North Atlantic Treaty Organization (NATO) bombing seemed to put the momentum back on the side of the rebels. Sirte, the last Gaddafi stronghold, fell on October 20, with Gaddafi's capture and death at the hands of the rebels.

The tragic thing about all this is that Libya is a country of immense natural and cultural wealth. Libya was the world's 12th-largest exporter of oil before the war broke out, and the quality of Libya's oil is an important factor, besides the sheer volume of production. Libya's "sweet light crude" oil is extremely low in sulfur content, which makes it highly desirable in global markets. It burns cleaner and is easier to refine into gasoline. Saudi Arabia offered to make up the shortfall during the height of the war, given that oil production in Libya had come to a halt, but oil from Saudi Arabia is "sour crude" with a high sulfur content that requires many more resources to refine it into usable petroleum.

Libya has the largest proven oil reserves in Africa, with 46.5 billion barrels of oil and over 46 trillion cubic feet (1.3 trillion cubic meters) of gas.

Before the war, Libya was Europe's single largest oil supplier, the second-largest oil producer in Africa, and the continent's fourth-largest gas supplier. Rising oil prices are viewed with anxiety by most countries, because they could jeopardize global economic recovery from a world economy that is still getting over the 2009 recession.

Libya is among the world's largest oil economies, with approximately 3.5 percent of global oil reserves, more than twice those of the United States. Libya has 10 times the proven oil reserves of Egypt and is the largest oil economy in the African continent, followed by Nigeria and Algeria. In contrast, U.S. proven oil reserves are on the order of 20.6 billion barrels. Foreign oil companies pulled out of Libya in late February when the civil war erupted there, triggering the shutdown of most of its oil production facilities.

Libya's rebels seek to restart crude production and generate the much-needed cash. At full capacity, the Arabian Gulf Oil Company, or Agoco, the Benghazi operator under rebel control, could pump up to 440,000 barrels a day, out of Libya's previous 1.6 million to 1.7 million barrels a day

A view of the Zawaiya Oil Refinery, located on the outskirts of the capital city of Tripoli.

capacity. Agoco said that it has maintained the infrastructure in good-enough condition to restart modest production, allowing it to ramp up over four months to full output at a cost of about $800 million. The National Transitional Council is keen to start sales of individual cargoes on the open market to fund the war effort and meet the unpaid salaries for public sector workers.

All this chaos has had a catastrophic effect on the lives of civilians in Libya. The United Nations Human Rights Council estimated that 25,000 people were killed during the civil war. Many states evacuated their citizens—China set up its largest evacuation operation ever, with 30,000 Chinese nationals being evacuated. Many international oil companies decided to withdraw their staff from Libya to ensure their safety. Fleeing the violence of Tripoli by road, as many as 4,000 refugees have been crossing the Libya—Tunisia border daily. These refugees were native Libyans as well as Tunisians, Egyptians, and Turks. The total Libyan refugee numbers were estimated at nearly one million as of June 2011. The World Health Organization has warned of the risks of epidemics at refugee camps. Hospital morgues are packed to the brim and medical supplies are running low.

The intense fighting in Libya has left the city of Sirte deserted and destroyed.

On March 17, 2011, the UN Security Council authorized a no-fly zone over Libya. A coalition of states began enforcing the no-fly zone from March 19, which greatly aided the rebels.

One positive result that has emerged from the war is that the Berbers (an ethnic group from north Africa), who had long been suppressed under Gaddafi, have come to the forefront as key players in this war. Berbers, in the Nafusa Mountains, said that they were inspired to wholeheartedly join the uprising when they saw the Arabs put aside decades of privileges that Gaddafi had bestowed upon them and join the rebellion that began in the country's east. Their language, which was suppressed for years, is now spoken openly again, and children even sing Berber songs. Gaddafi encouraged an Arab—Berber divide because it made it easier for him to rule the country, but the Arabs and Berbers united against him as a common enemy. However, the interim Libyan cabinet that was unveiled had no Berber representation, sparking fear in the Berber community that their culture would once again be undermined and sidelined.

RAMADAN

Although the Koran, the Muslim holy book, makes an exception, and specifically allows its holy warriors to drink and eat during Ramadan, the Muslim period of fasting, almost every rebel soldier on the frontlines of the Libyan civil war vowed that nothing would pass their lips from sunrise to sunset. Ramadan began on August 1, 2011, and lasted a month. There was no ceasefire. NATO officials said that they would continue to fly strike sorties over Libya, without pause. In Tripoli public frustration with Colonel Gaddafi deepened as power cuts were imposed throughout the city and residents went without air conditioning or refrigeration. There was also no cooking fuel and no gasoline for cars. This contributed to the widespread support for the rebels as they stormed into the city.

People are rejoicing now that this violent civil war is over. Hopefully Libya can rise from the ashes of this civil war, and the people can restore the infrastructure of society, and hold free and fair elections. People around the world are eager to see Libya reach full capacity in its production of "sweet crude" as soon as possible.

GEOGRAPHY

In the middle of Libya's mainly desert landscape springs Gaberoun Lake, an oasis lined with palms.

1

LIBYA IS LOCATED IN THE CENTER of the northern coast of the African continent. Tunisia and Algeria lie to the west, Niger and Chad to the south, and Egypt and Sudan to the east. Libya's 679,362 square miles (1,759,547 square kilometers) make it the fourth-largest country in Africa, one-fifth the size of the United States and slightly larger than the state of Alaska. Over 90 percent of it is desert, with rain falling only once every two to three years.

Libya has the longest Mediterranean coastline among African nations. Before the outbreak of the civil war, the beaches were a popular gathering place.

Over two-thirds of Libyans live on two narrow coastal strips near the Mediterranean Sea. Farther south there are scattered oasis settlements in the desert—a bare, dry world of sand and rock interrupted in places by pipelines. When the stretches of desert are included, Libya's average population density is only five people per square mile (three people per square km). Population density is about 130 persons per square mile (50 persons per square km) in the two northern regions of Tripolitania and Cyrenaica, but falls to fewer than 2.6 people per square mile (1 person per square km) elsewhere. Ninety percent of the people live in less than 10 percent of the area, primarily along the coast.

Libyans of the desert have developed a way of life that allows them to survive in a harsh world. Their most precious possessions are animals—camels, sheep, and goats—and their survival depends on the availability of water.

Families adopt a nomadic lifestyle, constantly on the move to find water holes and fresh grazing land for their herds. Unfortunately the unpredictable nature of the desert means that a water hole might be overflowing in one season and might go dry the next, so families never settle anywhere permanently.

THREE MAIN AREAS

Libya has three main regions: Tripolitania, Cyrenaica, and Fezzan. Until 1963 these regional names were the official names of provinces, but now they just indicate general geographic areas.

Tripolitania is Greek for "land of the three cities," in reference to Sabratha, Leptis Magna, and Oea (Tripoli). Its size is 110,000 square miles (284,900 square km), and it has a low, sandy coast that is occasionally fringed by lagoons. On the coastal Al-Jifarah Plain are salty marshes, sand dunes, and stretches of coarse grass, where wheat and barley are planted between rocky olive groves, together with fruit, cauliflower, tomatoes, and almonds.

The city of Tripoli has been the capital of Libya since its independence in 1951 from Italy. It is a fast-growing city, with new high-rise apartment buildings steadily taking the place of single-floor dwellings and improvised shanties. Palm trees and ornamental gardens fringe the Mediterranean shore, but any untended ground is hard and dusty.

Behind the coastal area, the land rises in a series of steps to the limestone ridge of Jabal Nafusah, which reaches a height of 2,500 feet (762 meters) in some places. Old craters and lava rocks indicate its volcanic origin. On the southern slopes, some figs and barley are grown, but the countryside is too dry to support much life. The area has been significant since before recorded history as a major population and cultural center of the Berber people, and it still shelters most of Libya's Berber-speaking population. On the bare, red sandstone plateau of Al Hamra' in northwestern Libya, desert nomads graze small herds of sheep and goats. In some places, attempts have been made to "pin down" the drifting sand with squared patterns of tough, rooted grass, and to plant species of fodder shrubs that can survive in dry areas.

To the east of this region are the Black Mountains, an unyielding wilderness of sharp, black basalt rock.

In February and March 2011, Tripoli witnessed intense antigovernment protests and violent government responses that resulted in hundreds of people getting killed and wounded. Green Square was the scene of some of the protests. The anti-Gaddafi protests were eventually crushed, and Tripoli has since been the site of pro-Gaddafi protests. In late February rebel forces took control of the city of Az Zawiyah, which is about 31 miles (50 km) to the west of the capital, thus increasing the threat to the forces loyal to Gaddafi in the capital. During the subsequent Battle of Az Zawiyah, loyalist forces besieged the city, and eventually recaptured it by March 10. Tripoli was taken by the rebels on August 23, 2011.

The capital city of Tripoli before the start of the civil war.

Cyrenaica (350,000 square miles, or 906,500 square km), Libya's other fertile coastal strip, has the towns of Benghazi and Tobruk. This area was once Greek, and the ruins of ancient Cyrene still attract visitors. Cyrenaica has been the center of the Libyan anti-Gaddafi forces in the 2011 Libyan civil war, with the National Transitional Council based in the city of Benghazi.

Inland the limestone plateau of the Green Mountains (Jabal Akhdar) reaches a height of 3,000 feet (914 m) in two slender strips, each only a few miles wide. In season the mountains are covered with a carpet of lilies, anemones, cyclamen, and narcissus. The higher parts have thick, thorny scrub, and there are patchy remains of juniper forests. Lotus grows in some of the damper southern valleys. The region is one of the very few forested areas of Libya, which is one of the least forested countries on Earth. It is the wettest part of Libya, receiving some 24 inches (60 centimeters) of precipitation annually. The high rainfall contributes to the area's large forests. It is an area

Camels in the hot, dry Sahara Desert.

that enjoys rich fruit, potato, and cereal agriculture, something of a rarity in the arid country.

THE LIBYAN DESERT

To the south of the Green Mountains lie the sweeping sand dunes and stony plateaus of the Libyan Desert. This arid region extends as far as southwestern Egypt and northwestern Sudan. Little can survive on these windswept, sunbaked plains of gravel. The temperature is seldom below 40°F (4°C) and frequently above 100°F (38°C).

There are scattered settlements, mostly oases with a few thousand inhabitants. Stores of underground water have been discovered at Al-Kufrah, allowing agriculture to begin to flourish. For centuries sweet water artesian wells in the Fayyum Oasis have permitted extensive cultivation in an irrigated area that extends over 811 square miles (2,100 square km).

The bulk of the southern part of Libya is loosely known as Fezzan (270,270 square miles, or 700,000 square km), although this name actually applies only to a depression about 300 miles (480 km) south of Tripoli. Located in Fezzan are two of the larger oasis settlements, Sabha and Murzuq. This is harsh desert country where life depends on springs and wells fed by underground water.

From the rock paintings discovered in the Sahara, it is clear that the region was once fertile, with enough pasture for large herds. Fezzan saw many traders traveling between the Phoenician—Roman coast and the rich areas of central Africa. Today occasional camel caravans still thread their way across wastelands of sand, from oasis to oasis, as they have done for centuries. One of the five ancient north—south routes goes through Sabha, where the path diverges to go southeast and southwest. A fort stands on a flat-topped hill some distance from Sabha. It once housed a French garrison

During World War II, the Libyan Desert became famous as the region of operations of the Siwa-based Long Range Desert Group, or LRDG, whose daring, vehicle-borne desert raids stretched as far west as Murzuk.

SAHARA DESERT

Not all desert is sand. In fact sand dunes cover only about a quarter of the 5.7 million square miles (9.1 million square km) of the Sahara, the second-largest desert in the world, after Antarctica. Much of the Sahara is covered by rock and gravel. Its highest parts are the Tassili N'ajjer in Algeria and the Tibesti Mountains, both touching the southern borders of Libya. Surrounding these mountains are plains of gravel formed partly from ancient river beds. Six thousand years ago, the Sahara was green. We know this from fossils found in the Sahara and from the Tassili cave paintings and engravings of antelopes, ostriches, elephants, and lions. The Sahara's ancient inhabitants progressed from hunting to herding. Later paintings show cattle, sheep, and goats. Perhaps, as is happening in other parts of Africa today, overgrazing followed by erosion started to transform the once-green land into desert. Diminishing rainfall accomplished the rest. Stretching from the Atlantic Ocean to the Red Sea, the Sahara contains mountains that reach up to 11,204 feet (3,415 m) in height; lost oases; forgotten cities; salt, iron, copper, and uranium mines; oil wells; and plains of multicolored rock, gravel, and sand.

but is now a police post. Most of Fezzan is flat, but a section of the Tibesti Mountains, mostly within Chad, Bikku Bitti, rises on the border to 7,440 feet (2,267 m)—the highest point in Libya.

The three sand seas, which contain dunes up to 1680 feet (512 m) in height, cover approximately one-quarter of the region.

CLIMATE

Within Libya five different climatic zones have been recognized, but the dominant climatic influences are Mediterranean and Saharan. Both the Mediterranean Sea and the desert affect Libya's climate. Most of the country has a desert climate, with an average annual rainfall of only 10 inches (25 cm), which falls intermittently between November and early May.

Around the cities of Tripoli and Benghazi, the rainfall may reach 14 inches (36 cm) a year, but the desert areas (94 percent of the country) receive less

The city of Medina in the Fezzan region.

than 4 inches (10 cm). Deficiency in rainfall is reflected in an absence of permanent rivers or streams, and the approximately 20 perennial lakes are brackish or salty.

Sabha, the main town of Fezzan, has been called the driest town in the world. Even in areas close to the Mediterranean, the summers are viciously dry and hot. Average winter temperatures vary from 52°F to 63°F (11°C to 17°C). Summer temperatures range from a low of 82°F (28°C) to a high of 100°F (38°C), but can rise to around 120°F (49°C). A world record of 136.4°F (58°C) was recorded in 1922 at Al Aziziyah, only 50 miles (80 km) southwest of Tripoli.

There are areas in the Libyan Desert where children grow to the age of 10 years or more without ever having experienced rain. Such areas are called the sand seas because there are no shrubs or stones, only sand. Sandstorms called *ghibli* (GIB-lee) sweep across the desert two or three times a year in what seems like a wall of wind and red sand up to 2,000 feet (610 m) high. The winds can raise the temperature by as much as 20°F (7°C) in a few hours, causing severe damage to crops. Along with the storms come a parching dryness and sand that clogs eyes, nose, and ears.

The winters can be bitterly cold and unpleasant. Frost—sometimes even sleet and snow—is common in the mountains, and the desert nights are chilling. The winter rains along the Gulf of Sirte coast can turn limestone dust from the surrounding desert into seas of mud that make travel slow or almost impossible.

The high inland ranges receive only an inch or two of light winter rain each year. This is enough for the scattered spiny shrubs to survive, providing grazing land for the hardy sheep and goats of many nomadic groups.

The northern shores of Africa, including the Nile Valley, were the grain-producing areas of the Roman Empire. In Libya more than 200 Roman wells have been discovered. Once cleaned, they work as well as they did 2,000 years ago. The Roman settlers and farmers dammed up narrow dry valleys known as wadis to trap moisture. Aqueducts 70 to 100 miles (110 to 160 km) long were built to carry water to the public baths in the thriving coastal cities.

There are no permanent rivers anywhere in Libya. If a rainstorm does occur, the streams that flow downhill to the valleys are soon lost in the dry earth. Droughts that last one to two years occur every five or six years.

WHAT LIVES IN THIS LAND?

In this dry climate, grass grows where it can. Esparto grass was once Libya's main export crop. It was used for making fine paper and rope. Herbs grow near the sea, including the asphodel lily, which the Greeks associated with death and planted on graves. Wild pistachios and henna shrubs that make a deep-red dye grow in the oases. The dye is used by North African women to paint designs on their hands and to tint their hair.

The most common animals in Libya are domesticated, including sheep, goats, cattle, horses, camels, and donkeys. Where there is sufficient shade and water, one can also see hyenas, jackals, and wildcats.

In the dry desert areas lies a wilderness empty of life during the day. Most lizards, snakes, and rodents would die in a few minutes in the hot sun; so dune creatures have learned to burrow underground, where it is cooler.

When the sun goes down and the sand cools, animals such as the jerboa come out to feed. With a tail almost as long as its 6-inch (15-cm) body, the mouse-like jerboa moves in a series of jumps with its forefeet held together, small carnivores such as fennecs (small foxes) watching for them. Fennecs

The nocturnal jerboa is a desert-dwelling rodent found in Libya.

obtain the water they need by eating jerboas as well as lizards and beetles.

Snakes and lizards are cold-blooded, meaning their blood temperature is not constant. At night their body temperature falls so low that in the morning, they must bask in the sun in order to bring their bodies back to normal working condition. During that time they are vulnerable to predators such as hawks and foxes. If they lie in the sun for too long, they overheat, so they soon dig their way underground for shelter.

The skink is a common desert lizard. It has a wedge-shaped jaw, handy for digging sheltering holes in loose sand, and its eyes are covered with transparent scales. It is sometimes called a sandfish because when it runs, it looks as if it is swimming through the sand.

Skinks are regarded as delicacies by the desert nomads, who gut and roast them on skewers. Skinks are small and easy to take care of, and children in towns sometimes keep them as pets.

Most of the desert gazelle have been hunted for food and skins, but there is one breed of antelope that can be found in small pockets in the Idhan Desert near the Algerian border. This is the lumbering addax antelope, which is highly endangered. It seems to survive without water. Nomads believe that the juice from the vegetable matter in the stomach of an addax can cure any illness, from scorpion bites to food poisoning.

WHAT'S BEING DONE?

In ancient times much of Libya was fertile. The Romans built elaborate irrigation systems, as the ruins of huge cisterns indicate. There were apparently abundant supplies of wheat, barley, citrus fruits, olives, and dates.

THE PALM TREE

In Libya, palm trees are found either by the sea or by most oases. It is never too hot or cold for the date palm, which survives night frosts and even snow. Date palms are either male or female. Pollen from a male tree is necessary for a female tree to produce fruit. The Bedouin believe palms that grow close together are friends. If one dies, the other trees will droop in mourning.

Nomads use every part of the date palm. The trunk provides timber, fuel, and fiber to make sacks and rope; the stalks are used for fences and roofs; the stringy part of the leaf is woven into baskets, mats, and sandals; and the juice of the young palm makes a sweet drink that can be fermented into palm wine. And, of course, there is the fruit. Dates are the nomad's daily bread. Dried and ground, they provide date flour, while their juice makes date honey. Even the date stones are ground and mixed with fodder for cattle or roasted to produce date coffee, a very bitter drink.

Libya's revolutionary leader Colonel Muammar Gaddafi once promised that "the desert will bloom." A three-year plan was launched in 1973, followed by a more ambitious five-year plan in 1976. The aim was to make fuller use of the natural resources, increase agricultural production, and create self-sufficient communities in agricultural areas. Nevertheless the country still imports 75 percent of its food.

In the coastal areas, small amounts of petroleum waste mixed with other products have been sprinkled on the surface of the sand dunes to prevent wind erosion. This has allowed eucalyptus trees to take root on the dunes. Coarse grass has been planted in square grids to prevent the sand from drifting.

In 1984 construction began on a pipeline more than 1,000 miles (1,610 km) long. Known as the Great Man-Made River, it was designed to bring water to northern Libya from deep underground reserves in the Sahara. However, it has not increased food production dramatically.

THE CAMEL

Although motorized transportation is common in Libya, the camel remains valuable for long journeys and is also used for plowing. A camel's speed rarely exceeds 4 miles (6 km) an hour. It can be forced into a rapid trot, but only for a few minutes or it will go lame. Owners look after camels carefully because to own many camels is a sign of great wealth.

The camel can drink 20 gallons (90 liters) of water at one time. But ignore rumors that this water is stored in its hump; the hump is made of fat and does not store water. The camel stores its main supply of liquid in its stomach, which has three sections and can hold over 50 gallons (225 l). When all that is used up, the camel goes on for two or three days on the liquid stored in its body tissues.

The camel is actually an Asiatic animal and was not introduced to the deserts west of the Nile River until the first century B.C. Known as the ship of the desert, the one-humped Arabian camel can survive on dry twigs and can smell water up to a mile away. It lives for 40 years or more, and can carry a load of 1,000 pounds (450 kilograms) and travel 25 miles (40 km) a day. The nomadic Libyans make use of every part of a camel carcass. Its thick hide is used to make sandals, and its hump provides lard. The meat of young camels is eaten and camel's milk is drunk and used to make cheese. Camel droppings are dried for fuel.

In biblical times, when the Hebrew nation under Gideon fought the various peoples of Canaan, the raiding Midianites that attacked the Israelites rode on camels. The sight of the raiders on these animals—creatures previously considered wild and untamable—frightened the mighty Hebrew soldiers. Even trained camels can be haughty and vicious; they spit, bite, and kick when they are annoyed.

Colonel Gaddafi's government constructed a network of dams in the wadis, dry watercourses that become torrents after heavy rains. These dams are used both as water reservoirs and for flood and erosion control. The wadis are heavily settled because soil in their bottoms is often suitable for agriculture, and the high water table in their vicinity makes them logical locations for digging wells. In many wadis, however, the water table is declining at an alarming rate, particularly in areas of intensive agriculture and near urban centers.

FEATHERED FOWL

The birds of Libya include eagles, hawks, vultures, wagtails, owls, ravens, black and white wheatears, partridges, and sandgrouse. Sandgrouse have special water-absorbent feathers that allow them to carry moisture back to their nest to cool their eggs. The noble falcon is seldom seen flying wild, though there are desert sheikhs who keep trained falcons for hunting small game or other birds.

The desert lark has a special place in nomadic tradition. Children are warned not to follow it. If they follow the lark a yard or two, and then a few more, they may easily get lost in the desert.

INTERNET LINKS

www.anglo-libyan.com/2006/12/libyas-endangered-animals.html

This website includes a lovely description and pictures of Libya's endangered wildlife.

www.mongabay.com/reference/country_studies/libya/GEOGRAPHY. html

This site provides a comprehensive description of the geography of Libya.

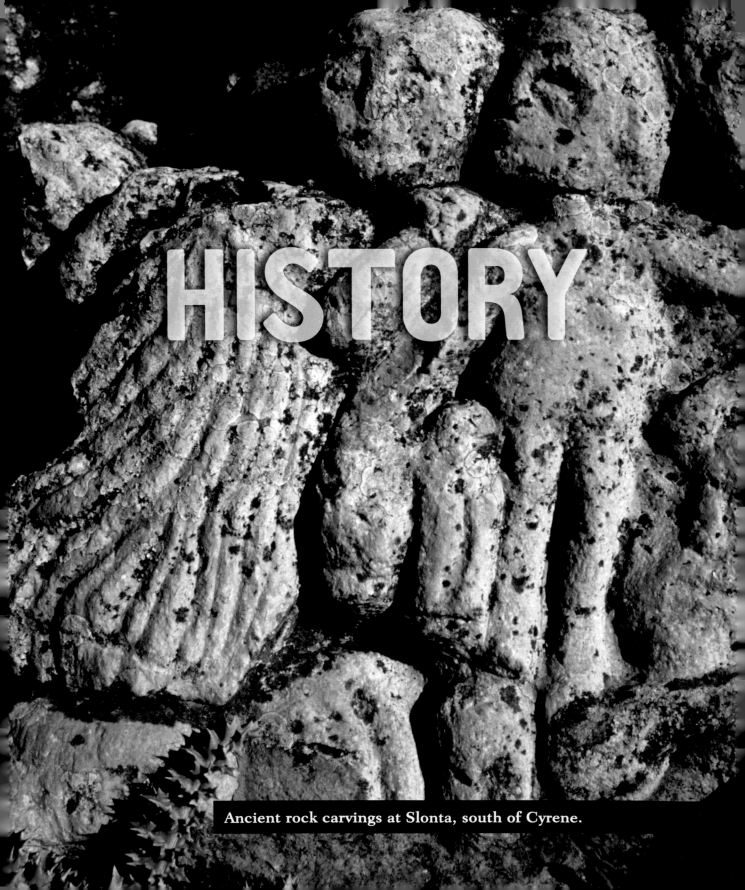

HISTORY

Ancient rock carvings at Slonta, south of Cyrene.

2

FOR HUNDREDS OF YEARS, THE name Libya referred to all of Africa except Egypt. To its Mediterranean shores came cautious visitors from different exploring nations. The oases in the interior and the few fertile areas were the settlements of Berber nomads some time before 2000 B.C.

From about 1000 B.C., Phoenician sailors from what is now known as Lebanon began to visit the North African coast in search of gold, silver, ivory, apes, and peacocks. They founded Carthage (in modern-day Tunisia), and Carthaginian ships and armies challenged the might of the Roman Empire. By then, the Greeks had founded the city of Cyrene (in the Al Jabar Al Akhdar region of present-day Libya), one of the cultural centers of the Greco-Roman world. Cyrene was a place of learning, where doctors and philosophers thrived. Wine, wool, and medicinal herbs were produced there. In 67 B.C. Cyrenaica, together with Crete, became a province of the Roman Empire.

The Romans destroyed Carthage in 146 B.C. and gained control of North Africa. Libya was developed into a useful grain-producing area. The Romans built the fine cities of Sabratha, Leptis Magna, and Oea in what is now Tripolitania.

After A.D. 435 Tripolitania fell into the hands of the Vandals and Byzantine Greeks before the Arab conquest in A.D. 642.

The Greeks and the Romans called all foreigners barbarians, meaning "babblers," because they spoke a language no Greek or Roman could understand. That is how the Berber people, living inland in the Sahara Desert and mountains, got their name. The Berbers, or Amazigh, controlled the caravan routes across Africa, using horse-drawn war chariots to terrify their foes. Although they paid taxes to Rome, they remained fiercely independent. A line of Roman-built forts, including Leptis Magna, built by Septimius Severus, protected the prosperous coastal cities. Even the Germanic Vandals, who broke up the Roman Empire in A.D. 410 and swept through Spain and the northern shores of Africa, never subdued the Berbers.

THE ARRIVAL OF ISLAM

Despite the success of Islamic armies in conquering North Africa, they had trouble defeating the Berbers, who were led by a chieftain named Kusaylah and later by a woman named Kahinah. It took the Arabs 15 years to finally overcome Berber resistance.

In the seventh century A.D., Islamic armies from the Middle East swept westward until they controlled all of North Africa and half of Spain. They brought with them their religion and language. The Arabs were not town dwellers, and the Roman cities were left to the enveloping sand, apart from the central area of Oea, which was maintained as a fort and on which the city of Tripoli now stands. There is still debate as to whether Islamic armies offered the inhabitants the choice of conversion to their religion, although Islam states that no one should be forced to convert.

After the death of the Prophet Muhammad, Islam's founder, rule over the Islamic conquests passed into the hands of the caliphs, the Prophet Muhammad's successors. Libya became part of the area controlled by the legendary Haroun al-Raschid of Baghdad. He appointed a local governor to rule from what is now Kairouan in Tunisia. In the struggles for power between successive caliphs, Libya changed allegiance to Egypt and then back to Baghdad.

In 1051 the Arabs in Tunisia, Tripolitania, and Cyrenaica rebelled against the powerful Fatimid caliphs of Cairo. Not only did the Fatimids send armies to subdue these provinces, but they also sent families and livestock to populate the area. This was the real Arab invasion of North Africa. The newcomers intermarried with the local people, and the Arabic language and way of life became a mainstay of Libyan culture.

For over 300 years, marauding fleets of pirates based in Tripoli made the North African coast feared by all who sailed the Mediterranean. They seized trading vessels in the Mediterranean, plundered the cargoes, and sold the crews into slavery. In Spain, where the Arab invaders had settled, Christian armies were gathering. In 1510 a European expedition captured Tripoli, and the Order of Knights of the Hospital of Saint John of Jerusalem sent a detachment of soldiers from Malta to build a castle there.

Ruins of a Byzantine church in Cyrene.

INVASION OF EMPIRE BUILDERS

Turkish Muslims from the Ottoman Empire invaded Libya in 1551. They captured Tripoli, encouraged pirate fleets to sail again, and even made expeditions against the Berbers inland. In 1799 the young United States of America began paying an annual tribute to the Turks to ensure safe passage for its ships. Turkish soldiers, called janissaries, also settled in Libya and married local women. Libya remained under Turkish influence for three centuries and buildings from the Turkish period still stand today.

In 1911 Italy declared war on Turkey and invaded Libya. Beneath the sand, the Italians found the impressive remains of cities built by their Roman ancestors. They felt they were returning to lands that had once been theirs. (Benito Mussolini was a newspaper editor at that time and strongly criticized the invasion. He was a socialist at that time. He was jailed for opposing the invasion. When he became the dictator of Fascist Italy, he counted Libya and Ethiopia as part of the "new empire.") There was a deliberate attempt by the Italian army to destroy Arab culture. Libyans in the occupied areas were given limited political rights, and those who refused to accept Italian authority were massacred.

After making the pilgrimage to Mecca, a Berber leader named Sheikh Muhammad ibn Ali al-Sanusi decided that Islam needed strengthening against the persuasive attractions of the Western world. He opened a series of religious lodges. The first was in Mecca, and another in Libya. By 1867 there were 50 lodges in Cyrenaica. The aim of the Sanusi Muslims was to live pious lives and purify their faith. In due course, this brotherhood of stern-minded Arabs made highly effective warriors against the Italians.

The Sanusi (sahn-OO-see) sect became the backbone of Libyan resistance. This was the time of the legendary Sanusi hero, Omar al-Mukhtar, a simple country schoolteacher who led the Libyan resistance. Leading a force of nomadic fighters that rose to 6,000 people, Omar led intermittent attacks on Italian communications and supply lines for nearly 20 years. In September 1931 he was wounded and captured in the Green Mountains and subsequently hanged before a crowd of 20,000 sad Libyans. During World War II, many Sanusis fled to Egypt and joined the Allied forces to continue the fight against the Italians.

Stories are still told of the Italian army's cruelty: how they sealed Bedouin wells, destroyed herds of cattle and drove people into concentration camps. The hanging of Libyans in every city became a daily event. Despite their unpopularity, more than 150,000 Italians settled in Libya.

TWO WORLD WARS

World War I made Italy loosen its grip on Libya for a brief period, as Italy was occupied with the war in Europe. Many World War II battles were fought across North Africa. The Desert War was a gigantic conflict that swept back and forth through Tunisia, Libya, and Egypt. The Allied armies and the Axis troops advanced and retreated as much as 4,000 miles (6,500 km). Britain's Eighth Army and Germany's Afrika Korps earned their fame as much from battling the Libyan Desert as from battling each other.

Much of the fighting revolved around the Libyan port of Tobruk. Long lines of gravestones in the desert form the military cemeteries of the Allied and Axis troops. Even today wandering camels and sometimes herdsmen are killed by one of the thousands of landmines that lie buried as deadly souvenirs of the Desert War.

After the war the victorious Allied powers realized Libya's strategic importance and argued for a long time about who should take over the land. But it seemed best to give Libya the chance to make its own choice. So, in 1951, the United Nations declared Libya an independent state, and a national assembly chose Muhammad Idris al-Sanusi as its first monarch.

MONARCHY

King Idris swiftly showed the style of rule he favored—absolute. There was one hotly contested election in 1952, after which Idris banned all political parties, banished most of his relatives to the desert, and deported the leader of the main opposition party. Though improvements were soon made in Libyan education and health services, the people in power became richer, while the poor remained poor.

As the Western world powers had hoped, Idris welcomed British and U.S. military bases into Libya. Wheelus Air Force Base near Tripoli became a main training base for the NATO and a part of the Western defense system. At the time of independence, Libya was poverty-stricken, and its people mostly illiterate. In return for the military bases, the United States and Great Britain provided substantial economic and technical aid.

One of the benefits of having foreign experts in Libya was the discovery of oil fields in the desert. By 1960 there were 35 oil wells in production. Exports of petroleum rose from 8,188,490 short tons (8 million metric tons) in 1962 to over 77,161,791 short tons (70 million metric tons) in 1966. Much of the profit went to the foreign countries that had done the drilling. Unfortunately little of Libya's newfound wealth was passed to those who needed it.

As the king's health began to fail, corruption in his government increased. Many Libyans wished for a new government. Some had been planning for many years to organize a coup.

The United Nations Education, Scientific, and Cultural Organization (UNESCO) has urged all sides involved in the fighting to preserve Libya's cultural heritage. Libya has five UNESCO World Heritage sites:

LEPTIS MAGNA *Leptis Magna was enlarged and embellished by Septimius Severus, Roman emperor from A.D. 193 to 211. He was born there and later became emperor. It was one of the most beautiful cities of the Roman Empire, with its imposing public monuments, harbor, marketplace, storehouses, shops, and residential districts. Although Leptis (a Latinized version of its Phoenician name) was comparable to the other Phoenician trading centers of the Syrian coast, like Sabratha, after Septimius Severus became emperor in A.D. 193, its fortunes improved remarkably. Thanks to him, the renewed Leptis became one of the most beautiful cities of the Roman world. It is still one of the best examples of Severan urban planning. The ancient port, with its artificial basin of some 1.1 million square feet (102,000 square m), still exists with its quays, jetties, fortifications, storage areas, and temples. The market, an essential element in the everyday life of a large commercial trading center, with its votive arch, colonnades, and shops, has been preserved for the most part.*

CYRENE *Cyrene was the ruins of the Greeks coming from the island of Thera. It was one of the main cities of ancient Greece. The ruins are located in the valley, in the Jebel Akhdar uplands, in the present-day city of Shahhat in Libya. Cyrene was founded by the Greeks in 630 B.C. It grew to become one of the major cities of ancient Libya, establishing trade relations with other Greek cities of that period. It had its own kings in the fifth century B.C., but by 460 B.C it had become a republic. Cyrene was conquered by the Romans around 96 B.C., and was made a Roman province. Under the Romans, Cyrene remained an important city until it came to an unceremonious end in a massive earthquake that took place in A.D. 262.*

SABRATHA *The archaeological site of Sabratha (pictured right on next page) contain the ancient ruins in northwestern Libya. Sabratha was established by the Phoenicians* around 500 B.C. as a trading post for products coming from the African hinterland. It was originally called Sbrt'n. There is a possibility that a village might have already existed in the area when the Phoenicians arrived.

OLD TOWN OF GHADAMES *The old town of Ghadames stands in an oasis and is known as the pearl of the desert. The town is the one of the oldest pre-Saharan settlements and while none of its original buildings remain, it still retains its domestic architectural style. Houses were organized vertically by function—ground floors were used to store supplies, an upper floor for family, and open-air terraces reserved for women.*

ROCK-ART SITES OF TADRART ACACUS *Tadrart Acacus is located in a mountainous region, located in the Fezzan, east of the city of Ghat. Thousands of cave paintings in varying styles can be found on cave walls scattered throughout the region. The paintings date from 12,000 B.C. to A.D. 100 and reflect the changes of plant and animal life and also depict the changing ways of life of people who lived in the region.*

THE REVOLUTION

In the early morning of September 1, 1969, while King Idris was on vacation in Turkey, Libyan army officers captured the state palace in Tripoli in a bloodless coup. A few hours later, the leader of the coup, Muammar Abu Minyar al-Gaddafi, seized a radio station in Benghazi and broadcast the news. He told listening Libyans that the monarchy had been replaced by a republic. Many Libyan army units had wanted to seize control for months, but Gaddafi's group acted first.

The king expected the United States or Great Britain to restore him to the throne. But neither nation wished to stir up trouble in the Middle East. Idris soon announced that he was passing the throne on to his son, Crown Prince Hassan al-Reda. The prince was promptly arrested and hastily agreed to urge Libyans to support the new regime. Idris went into exile in Egypt where he died in 1983.

In an interview with an Egyptian editor, Gaddafi expressed the hope that Egypt's president, Gamal Abdel Nasser, whom Gaddafi admired greatly, would take over the country. When that did not happen, Gaddafi promoted himself as colonel and was automatically accepted as chairman of the new government. At the age of 27 years he became the ruler of Libya. His main aims quickly became apparent: to build unity among the Arab countries, to create a Libyan socialist republic based on Islamic law, and to destroy Israel, which he regarded as the prime enemy of the Arab world.

THE LONE FALCON

Gaddafi was born to a family of desert nomads. As one of his grandfathers had been killed by the Italian invaders, and his father and uncle imprisoned for resisting them, young Gaddafi learned to hate Europeans at an early age.

By the age of 10 years, his teachers recognized that he was remarkably intelligent. He rose to the top of his class and was promoted swiftly. One of his early fascinations was the radio. He would listen to it for hours, often going without food so that he could buy new batteries. The Voice of the

Arabs programs broadcast from Egypt allowed Gaddafi to listen to President Nasser, who became his hero.

While attending high school in Sabha, Gaddafi began to recruit secret cells of students with the plan to overthrow the Libyan monarchy. The plan leaked and Gaddafi was expelled. Undaunted, he attended another school, graduated with honors, and entered the University of Libya. He continued planning to overthrow the king. After earning a degree in law, he joined the army and steadily recruited more followers. By August 1969 Gaddafi was the acting adjutant of the Libyan Signal Corps. With most of Libya's 7,000-strong army already sympathetic to the revolutionary cause, he launched the coup on September 1, 1969.

Four months after the coup, Gaddafi married a teacher at a midnight ceremony attended by Nasser. The marriage failed and they divorced after the birth of one son. In July 1970 Gaddafi married a nurse, who bore him more children.

Gaddafi created controversy in the Middle East and beyond. After Nasser died in 1970, his successor, Anwar Sadat, did not share Gaddafi's dream for Arab unity. This led to the deterioration of relations with Egypt. When Sadat tried to make peace with Israel, Gaddafi rallied several Arab states to freeze relations with Egypt. On the international stage, he astounded politicians and rulers with his lack of tact. On the domestic front, Italians in Libya were expelled in 1970, and an American airbase, the Wheelus base, was vacated in June 1970 and returned to Libyan control.

Obsessed with power and the desire for perfection in his country, Gaddafi instituted the death penalty for anyone who dared to engage in political activity against him. Strikes were forbidden. The Arab Socialist Union became Libya's only political party. To support his ideals, Gaddafi produced the *Green Book* in three volumes, setting out his theories for the perfect democracy, the perfect economy, and the way of life that he called the Third Universal Way. He had three unshakable obsessions: revolution, Islam, and Arab unity.

In an effort to show that he was still a humble Arab at heart, Gaddafi declared his only title as "Brother Colonel." He was photographed in his family

A picture of Muammar Gaddafi taken in 1973.

"We will teach how a people can take up arms to stage a revolution."
—Muammar Gaddafi

On April 15, 1973, the day on which the Prophet Muhammad's birthday was being celebrated, the announcement of Libya's new Cultural Revolution was made. It was designed to uphold the ideals of the Al-Fatah revolution (in 1969, when Gaddafi came to power) and give the country to its people. It was also a further excuse to purge the country of any dissident elements. To expel communists and capitalists is one thing; to imprison thousands of peaceful Libyans who happen to disagree is another altogether.

Arabic was made the official language by a Revolutionary Committee firmly guided by Gaddafi. Anything printed in English or Italian was removed. Following strict Islamic law, alcohol, revealing clothes, bars, casinos, and unsuitable literature were banned. Hundreds of books were burned.

Nevertheless the ordinary person in Libya found that the general quality of life began to improve. Roads, hospitals, and schools were built. Irrigation projects were planned to increase food production. The factories and assets of foreign companies were nationalized by the state. By 1977 Libya was the richest country on the African continent.

tent wearing Arab robes, although his usual dress was an army uniform. He roamed the streets in disguise, sharing the talk of the Libyan people. Slightly built with a deep, quiet voice and boyish grin, he walked with bent shoulders and hands in his pockets.

INTERNATIONAL TERRORISM

Certain that Libya had taken the right step toward freedom, Gaddafi began to support other insurgent movements around the world. In the 1970s and 1980s Libyan wealth backed terrorists in Northern Ireland, the Palestine Liberation Organization, the Basque separatist movement in Spain, and South African black activists fighting apartheid. In 1979 Gaddafi sent troops to support the brutal dictator Idi Amin in Uganda. It is suspected that there may have been as many as 20 camps in Libya training more than 7,000 terrorists for subversive activities around the world.

In 1988 Libya was believed to have been involved in the bombing of a commercial airplane in the skies over Lockerbie, Scotland, in which hundreds of people were killed. When Gaddafi refused to hand over the two Libyans suspected in the bombing, many countries severed diplomatic ties with Libya.

In 1992 the United Nations imposed sanctions on Libya for its continued harboring of the two suspects. In 1999 Gaddafi finally agreed to let the men stand trial in the Netherlands under Scottish law, and the UN sanctions were suspended. The trial came to an end in 2001, with one suspect jailed and the other set free. In August 2003 Libya admitted responsibility for the Lockerbie incident and the United Nations agreed to lift sanctions. However, the United States continued to boycott relations with Libya.

FOREIGN POLICY

In the 1980s the prime targets of Gaddafi's aggression were Israel and South Africa—the first seen as anti-Arab, and the other anti-black.

When South Africa reverted to majority black rule, Libya renewed diplomatic relations with the country. However, Libya has rejected the Middle East peace process, and no Libyan is allowed to travel to Israel, and vice versa.

In March 1986 U.S. warships deliberately sailed into the Gulf of Sirte, which Gaddafi had claimed as Libyan waters. Libya instantly launched an attack that backfired—Libyan vessels were sunk or damaged. Days later a series of terrorist attacks around the world seemed to implicate Libya. The United States launched an air attack on Tripoli and Benghazi, hoping to kill Gaddafi. The attack failed, but Gaddafi's adopted daughter was killed.

THE LIBYAN CIVIL WAR

The roots of the Libyan civil war began on February 15, 2011, as a series of peaceful protests that were met with military force by the Gaddafi regime.

The protests escalated into an uprising that spread across the country, with the forces opposing Gaddafi establishing a government based in Benghazi named the National Transitional Council whose goal was to overthrow the Gaddafi-led government and hold democratic elections.

The United Nations Security Council passed an initial resolution freezing the assets of Gaddafi and 10 members of his inner circle, and restricting their travel. The resolution also referred the actions of the government to the International Criminal Court for investigation, and an arrest warrant for Gaddafi was issued on June 27. In early March, Gaddafi's forces rallied, pushed eastward, and re-took several coastal cities before attacking Benghazi. A further UN resolution authorized member states to establish and enforce a no-fly zone over Libya. The Gaddafi government then announced a ceasefire, but failed to uphold it. The civil war is viewed as a part of the Arab Spring, which resulted in the ousting of long-term presidents of adjacent Tunisia and Egypt, with the initial protests all using similar slogans.

Medical supplies, fuel, and food have run dangerously low in Libya. On February 25, 2011, the International Committee of the Red Cross (ICRC) launched an emergency appeal for $6.4 million to meet the emergency needs of people affected by the violent unrest in Libya.

Migrants constituted 10.5 percent of the population of Libya in 2010. Migrants began trying to escape the Libyan crisis as violence escalated in the country. When migrants started to exit the country for the Egyptian and Tunisian borders, the International Organization for Migration began immediate evacuation operations for stranded migrants at international borders.

Fleeing the violence of Tripoli by road, as many as 4,000 refugees crossed the Libya—Tunisia border daily during the first days of the uprising. Among those escaping the violence were native Libyans as well as foreign nationals, including Egyptians, Tunisians, and Turks. In February the Italian foreign minister, Franco Frattini, expressed his concern that the number of Libyan refugees trying to escape to Italy might reach 200,000—300,000 people. By March 1 officials from the United Nations High Commissioner for Refugees had confirmed allegations of discrimination against sub-Saharan Africans who were being held in dangerous conditions in the no-man's-land between Tunisia and Libya. By March 3 an estimated 200,000 refugees had fled Libya to either Tunisia or Egypt. The International Criminal Court has estimated that 10,000 Libyans had been killed in the conflict as of March 7, 2011. The National Transitional Council estimates that about 25,000 Libyans perished as of October 2, 2011.

The capital city of Tripoli fell to the rebels on August 23, 2011. Gaddafi and his family fled the capital and were eventually captured when his convoy traveling to Sirte was caught in a NATO airstrike. Gaddafi took refuge in a large drainage pipe but was found, captured, and then killed. Gaddafi's controversial and brutal killing was captured on video, and conflicting accounts about the events leading to his death were reported. Several international organizations, including the United Nations, as well as the U.S. and U.K. governments, are concerned that Gaddafi's death might have been an extrajudicial killing and have called for investigations into the events of his death.

INTERNET LINKS

www.bbc.co.uk/news/world-africa-13860458

This clear and concise website by the BBC contains color photographs explaining the origins of the civil war and the events that have unfolded so far, and explains the Libyan crisis.

www.npr.org/2011/03/07/134336993/Libyas-History-Sheds-Light-On-Current-Conflict

This site provides a radio interview with Cambridge University's George Joffe and Chuck Cecil, former U.S. liaison officer in Libya, about how Libya's history has given rise to the current conflict. It includes both an audio file and soundtrack.

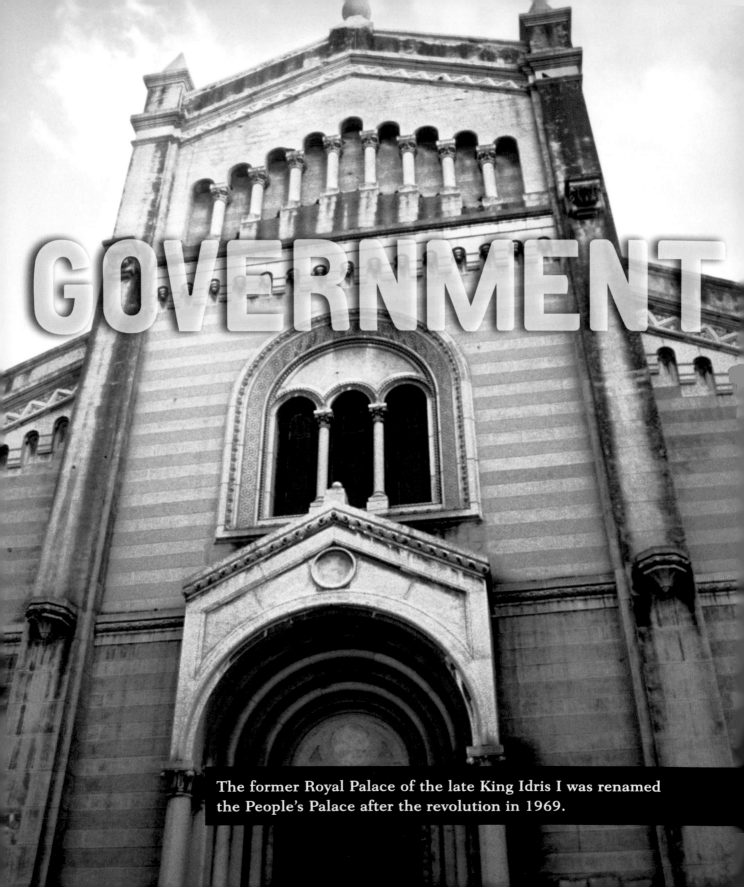

GOVERNMENT

The former Royal Palace of the late King Idris I was renamed the People's Palace after the revolution in 1969.

FROM ITS DAYS AS A COLLECTION OF scattered towns and tribes dominated by the Ottoman Empire and then the Italians, Libya became a modern nation that first gained an independent government in 1951. The rule of King Idris proved to be a dictatorship. He took all power into his own hands and banished those who offered any threat or opposition.

The new constitution approved by the United Nations in 1951 set up an elected house of representatives with 55 members and an upper house or senate, half of whom were nominated by the king. The king also had the power to appoint his own provincial governors, to veto legislation, and to dissolve the lower house completely if he so wished.

Within two years all political parties were banned. Idris made no attempt to meet the desires of his people by changing Libya from a monarchy (rule by a king or queen) to a republic (rule by an elected president).

The king's unpopularity became the grounds for revolution. The coup in September 1969 left Idris in exile and put Gaddafi in power. A 12-man revolutionary council was appointed, with Gaddafi as chairman. Libya was proclaimed "an Arab democratic and free republic." Ethnic leaders soon lost much of their power, and traditional interior boundaries ceased to exist. There is now only one political party: the Arab Socialist Union, formed in 1971, which allows all Libyans to participate in the government through their local popular congresses.

3

As a result of the Libyan civil war, the Benghazi-based National Transitional Council uses the name of Libya for the Libyan state, but has also on occasion referred to it as the Libyan Republic. It is led by Mustafa Abdul Jalil and controls most of the eastern half of the country.

In March 1977 the General People's Congress renamed the country the Socialist People's Libyan Arab Jamahiriya. (*Jamahiriya* is a word invented by Gaddafi, meaning a state of the masses.) With all power delegated to various committees, Libya claimed to be the first and only country in the world with "no government." People learned to talk of "the authorities" rather than "the government."

THE GREAT *GREEN BOOK*

Between 1976 and 1979 Gaddafi produced his three-volume *Green Book*, outlining his "final solution to the problem of governing" in three points:

1. The solution to the problems of democracy is to give authority to the people. Democracy is not government; it is the formation of committees everywhere, and "supervision of the people by the people."
2. The solution to economic problems is socialism. People should be "partners, not wage workers." They should control the places where they work and own homes.
3. The solution to social problems is the Third Universal Theory. This emphasizes the importance of family and tribal unity, the role of women (slightly inferior to men, and primarily to marry, and bear and raise children), the protection of minorities, and "how the blacks will prevail in the world."

The late Muammar Gaddafi at a United Nations General Assembly in 2009.

According to Gaddafi, these theories were intended to steer Libya away from the evils of Western-style democracy with its free-market capitalism and Marxist communism with its all-powerful politburo.

THE LAW

Although the country is run by the General People's Congress (a body of some 1,000 members formed from elected and appointed bodies), everyday life in Libya is ruled by strict Islamic law.

"Racism, barbarism, and savagery are deep-rooted in the ethics of the Western imperialist colonialists. . . . They are determined that African unity will not be established."

"All the efforts [of the Organization of African Unity] should be directed to the liberation of Palestine and South Africa, and the destruction of the racist regimes."

"We have given training to thousands of Africans—on Libyan soil—who took part in the liberation of a number of African countries."

The sacred law of Islam is called *Shari'ah* (SHARI-ya), which means "the path of Allah's commandments." *Allah* is the Arabic word for "God." Shari'ah is sometimes summarized as:
- what God has commanded
- what God has recommended
- what God has left for us to choose
- what God disapproves of
- what God has forbidden

The Shari'ah courts deal with family matters and business and property claims. Islamic law, if fully enforced, threatens such punishments as the amputation of a thief's hands.

There is also a criminal code of justice in Libya based mainly on the Egyptian model that has judges and a court of appeal. But all family matters are settled according to Islamic law, which originates from the Koran.

In small towns an ethnic leader or a respected priest, or imam, may be regarded as the governor of the town, but elected leaders date back to the Ottoman period.

Libyan soldiers marching during a military parade.

The Libyan armed forces played an important role in politics. They have many officers who hold key positions on many of the popular committees.

During the 1980s the zealous revolutionary committees terrorized the country. Thousands were arrested on suspicion. In addition to many being arrested, many left the country in permanent exile. These Libyans (young in the 1980s) have been essential participants, even from afar, in the uprising of 2011.

As a result the General People's Congress (GPC) was formed and given supreme power in the government. It had the power to sign treaties and declare war with other countries. The Congress elects the General People's Committee, the cabinet, and the revolutionary head or head of state.

The GPC also approved a charter of human rights, promising freedom of expression and condemning violence. Gaddafi's popularity with the masses increased as a result. The army and police force were abolished and replaced by a force of Jamahiriya Guards supervised by people's defense committees.

In August 1989 it was announced that the traditional armed forces had been abolished. In the future, they would be known as the armed people. That did not put an end to military service. Libyan men are still required to train for three years in the army or four years in the navy or air force.

In 2002 Libya's armed forces were estimated to number 76,000. The 50,000-strong army, of which 40,000 were reservists in the People's Militia, was equipped with Russian-made tanks. The navy, with 8,000 personnel, had two Russian F-class submarines and various frigates and coastal patrol crafts. The air force, employing 18,000 people, had more than 400 Russian- and French-made combat aircraft and 56 attack helicopters.

For all Gaddafi's well-publicized statements that military power was in the hands of the people, there were still many uniforms in the streets and plenty of military personnel on the most powerful committees. The original revolutionary council of army officers is no more, but most Libyans still consider the country a military state. An elaborate state security system penetrates all Libyan life. Before Gaddafi's death in 2011, there were at least nine coup attempts to remove him from power. The regime's human rights record is full of reports of torture, disappearances, and executions of anyone believed to pose a threat to the dictator's regime.

PEOPLE'S CONGRESS

Libya is strongly socialist. The government in Libya works through a national network of congresses and committees that are democratically elected by every citizen over the age of 18 years, whether male or female. In other words, ordinary people are encouraged and expected to play their part in government.

More than 2,000 of the local People's Congresses appoint higher-ranked Popular Committees that send resolutions to the GPC. These, in turn, pronounce the will of the people. National policy is directed by the GPC and administered by a series of secretariats. Each secretariat sends a secretary to the GPC, in much the same way as a cabinet in other democratic countries is made up of ministers from the different departments of government.

Though the political and economic capital of Libya is Tripoli, since 1988 all but two of the secretariats of the GPC have been relocated to other parts of the country.

NATIONAL TRANSITIONAL COUNCIL

The National Transitional Council (NTC) was formed on February 27, 2011, by former Libyan minister of justice, Mustafa Abdel Jalil. Its formation was announced in the city of Benghazi on February 27, 2011, and its intended purpose is to act as the "political face of the revolution." On March 5, 2011, the council issued a statement in which it declared itself to be the "only legitimate body representing the people of Libya and the Libyan state."

The council's main aims are to: ensure the safety of the national territory and citizens; coordinate national efforts to liberate the rest of Libya; support the efforts of local councils to work for the restoration of normal civilian life; supervise the military council to ensure the achievement of the new doctrine of the Libyan People's Army in the defense of the people and to protect the borders of Libya; facilitate the election of a constituent assembly to draft a new constitution for the country; form a transitional government to pave

Libya's interim cabinet was revealed on November 24, 2011.

the holding of free elections; guide the conduct of foreign policy, and the regulation of relations with other countries and international and regional organizations, and the representation of the Libyan people.

An executive board, chaired by Mahmoud Jibril, was formed by the council on March 23, 2011. The council has so far been officially recognized by 32 countries as the legitimate governing authority in Libya until general elections can take place. The council has established the following commercial bodies to manage its financial affairs: the Central Bank of Benghazi (to act as the "monetary authority competent in monetary policies in Libya"), and the Libyan Oil Company (to act as the "supervisory authority on oil production and policies in the country.")

With the death of Gaddafi, the NTC now plans to hold a Public National Conference by June 2012. After being elected, the Conference will select a new prime minister, cabinet, and constituent authority who will then draw up a new constitution that will be put to a referendum. Once the referendum is approved, general elections will take place.

INTERNET LINKS

http://online.wsj.com/article/SB10001424052748704629104576190 720901643258.html

This site provides an interesting article about the new leadership in Libya.

www.monstersandcritics.com/news/africa/news/article_1625037. php/PROFILE-Provisional-rebel-government-leader-Mustafa-Abdel-Jalil

This is one of the first websites about the provisional rebel government leader Mustafa Abdel Jalil.

www.ntclibya.org/english/

This is the Libyan National Transitional Council's official website.

ECONOMY

A young Libyan man picking olives from a grove in Zlitan, on the outskirts of Tripoli.

4

FOR CENTURIES LIBYA WAS ONE OF the poorest countries in the world. Farming produced just enough for people to live on, and the vast stretches of desert were not very useful to anyone except the nomads.

POVERTY TO WEALTH

In 1959 the discovery of oil changed Libya's fortunes. The increase in the price of oil in the 1970s made Libya the richest country in Africa. The oil industry provided employment and a high income for many Libyans.

The Central Bank of Libya.

However, the U.S. trade embargo with Libya, which began in 1982, and the UN sanctions in 1992 had a devastating effect on the economy. The standard of living declined rapidly and basic materials and food became scarce. Gaddafi's attempts to make Libya self-sufficient met with little success and although a few countries continued to trade with Libya, there was widespread discontent. When the United Nations suspended sanctions in 1999, life for Libyans improved as the economy began to recover.

Libya's rapid population growth reduced the overall wealth of the country. The population has climbed to 6.3 million, and if the current growth rate continues, the economy will not be able to provide enough jobs for young Libyans.

PETROLEUM

Libya's deserts conceal the largest underground reserves of oil in Africa and the eighth largest in the world. The reserves amount to about 30 billion barrels of oil. Libyan crude oil is particularly popular because it has little sulfur; it causes less pollution and is less expensive to process into petroleum. The nickname for such oil is "sweet crude."

In the 1960s, when these reserves were first tapped, Libya was the greatest oil producer in Africa. By 1965 Libya was the sixth-largest exporter in the world, and in 1969 its oil output exceeded even that of Saudi Arabia. Libya's oil production was severely restricted as a result of UN trade sanctions, but since the sanctions were suspended in 1999, many European and Arab countries have resumed drilling and refining operations in the country. The countries include Saudi Arabia, South Korea, Germany, Italy, Spain, and Canada.

Gaddafi invested heavily in Libya's oil refineries and pipelines. Oil and petroleum products made up more than 97 percent of exports and account for a large number of jobs in industry and construction. Libya had three refineries capable of handling about 340,000 barrels a day. Pipelines up to 180 miles (290 km) long stretch from the oil fields, mostly in the desert off the Gulf of Sirte, to tanker terminals on the coast.

During the Iran—Iraq War in the 1980s, oil prices skyrocketed, only to collapse in 1986. Although by that time all Libyan oil had been nationalized so no foreign company could make a profit, the drop in price badly affected Libya's economy. Fresh reserves of offshore oil and natural gas were found near Benghazi in the 1990s. They contributed further to Libya's oil wealth. It is possible that the present oil reserves in Libya could run out within the next 50 years. When the anti-government protests erupted, Libya was the 12th-largest oil exporter in the world.

Libya, an OPEC (Organization of Petroleum Exporting Countries; an intergovernmental group made up of twelve countries) member, was Africa's fourth-largest oil producer after Nigeria, Algeria, and Angola. It produced up to 1.8 million barrels per day and holds estimated reserves of 42 billion barrels. Eighty percent of its "sweet crude" exports are sold to European countries such as France, Germany, and particularly Italy. Since the start of the civil war, oil production was cut by half. During the war, the price per barrel shot up to a two-and-a-half-year high amid investor fears of a drop in production. Libya's "sweet crude" oil cannot be easily replaced in the production of gasoline, diesel, and jet fuel, particularly by the many European and Asian refineries that are not equipped to refine "sour" crude, which is higher in sulfur content.

Before the outbreak of the civil war, Libya was one of the largest producers of oil. The war caused the country to halve its production, and also destroyed infrastructure instrumental to the industry.

Many of essential pipelines were heavily damaged during the conflict and oil exports came virtually to halt. It is expected that repairs to the sector's infrastructure will cost hundreds of millions of dollars. Exports only resumed in September 2011. Oil production in Libya is now rising and the country's National Oil Corporation expects crude oil output to return to prewar levels (1.6 million barrels per day) by the end of 2012.

INDUSTRY

Libya boasts iron and steel complexes, an aluminum plant, and chemical complexes for natural salts. The most important industries in the public sector are processed foods (popular local products include canned tomato paste and tuna), soft drinks, tobacco, clothing, footwear, leather, wood, chemicals, and metal goods. Although in the past many factories were small and did not employ more than a hundred people, with heavy investment in large-scale complexes, industry now supports 29 percent of the workforce. Esparto grass is a commercial crop, and a state-controlled factory processes it for export. There are also factories making rugs and cloth from imported materials.

The emphasis on petroleum and industry has resulted in an increase in the number of Libyans living near Tripoli and Benghazi. Both these cities are surrounded by slums as well as military installations. The population drift to the towns has caused serious problems. As in other countries, urban migration has led to housing shortages, and health and lifestyle have suffered. As there are not enough skilled laborers, Libya requires many foreign workers, who often demand the best salaries and houses.

Since Libya's rebel uprising began in February 2011, the country's industrial production has ground to a halt. Libyans now rely extensively on neighboring Tunisia and Egypt for their food imports. The industrial city of Sfax in Tunisia is getting a boost from its neighbor, Libya. However, the Libyan revolution has had a twofold impact on Tunisia. Many Tunisian businesses have been forced to close their operations in Libya. Critical remittances have dried up as thousands of Tunisian workers headed home. And this small North African country is overwhelmed by thousands of refugees who fled Libya.

AGRICULTURE

Although agriculture is the second-largest sector in the economy, Libya depends on imports in most foods. Climatic conditions and poor soils limit farm output, and domestic food production meets about 25 percent of demand. However, things changed after the discovery of oil. The petroleum business produced get-rich-quick dreams among Libyans. There has been a growing flood of migrants from the farms to the towns. In 1960 about 70 percent of the population worked on the land; today the figure stands at less than 17 percent. Even the commercial farmers live in city houses and travel out each day to their farms on the Al-Jifarah Plain.

Less than 2 percent of the land is arable, and less than 4 percent is suitable for raising livestock. Farming produces only 7 percent of Libya's gross domestic product, and the yield per acre is the lowest of all North African countries. Nevertheless improved irrigation has brought more areas under cultivation, and farmers are encouraged to use cooperative methods. The main crops are wheat, olives, barley, dates, peanuts, and citrus fruits. All are grown near the coast except dates and figs, which are grown in the oases. There are serious shortages of flour, rice, and non-citrus fruits. Although Libya has nearly 1,118.5 miles (1,800 km) of coastline and the second-largest continental shelf in the Mediterranean, its waters are not particularly rich in plankton needed to sustain fishing waters. In fact, Libya has had to import most of its food due to the underdevelopment of agriculture. The civil war has not been kind to the agricultural sector, with most activities grinding to a halt.

Irrigation has enabled more areas in Libya to become arable.

SOUK TO SUPERMARKET

If you go shopping in Tripoli, you will notice the absence of valuable articles such as handcrafted metalwork, quality leather goods, and Persian carpets. The gold jewelry for which Tripoli became famous is no more. Shoppers can look in vain for the Souk of the Perfumers or the Souk of the Saddlers and Leatherworkers. The principal imports are food products such as sugar, tea, and coffee, as well as construction materials and consumer goods.

In 1981 Gaddafi tried to close all privately owned shops. He considered merchants "parasites" who produced nothing themselves but made

THE GREAT MAN-MADE RIVER

The Great Man-Made River is a network of pipes that supplies water to the coastal cities and towns in Libya, from the Nubian Sandstone Aquifer System fossil aquifer. It is the world's largest irrigation project.

It is the largest underground network of pipes (1,752 miles/2,820 km) and aqueducts in the world. It consists of more than 1,300 wells, most of these more than 1,640 feet (500 m) deep, and supplies 239 million cubic feet (6.5 million cubic m) of fresh water per day to the cities of Tripoli, Benghazi, Sirte, and elsewhere. Gaddafi described it as the "Eighth Wonder of the World."

Although the Great Man-Made River is impressive, experts think that the water table in the areas from which the water is being pumped may drop, threatening the supply to local oases. There is little hope of these deep water reserves being replenished if depleted. The thick, sandy dunes of the Sahara have so far protected underground water supplies from evaporation, but there is not sufficient rainfall to replenish them if they disappear. Within a century they could run dry.

money from the masses. So he encouraged the workers to seize control. They did. Most businesses with more than five employees are now controlled by a workers' committee. Gaddafi wanted people to shop only at state-registered supermarkets.

The system failed badly. Poor organization and interference by state committees caused bottlenecks in supply. Basic goods became unobtainable. Shopping was done on the black market. Gigantic state factories continued to create expensive goods nobody wanted to buy. In 1983 more than two-thirds of the country's food had to be imported; this included 800,000 tons of cereals. By 1985 Gaddafi was urging Libyans to eat camel meat to reduce the amount of beef and mutton being imported. It is hardly surprising that one of Libya's present aims is to be self-sufficient in food production.

Eventually the lack of small businesses was recognized as a problem, and in 1988 the private sector (mostly partnerships offering employment to a community) was reestablished. Many businesses reopened and food products were easier to find, but it was not enough to ensure a steady supply of goods to the cities. More than two decades later, Libya still imports 75 percent of its food.

TRANSPORTATION

Overall 29,571 miles (47,590 km) of Libya's 51,698 miles (83,200 km) of road are paved. Most Libyans travel by bus. Cars are very expensive because they are all imported. U.S.-made vehicles are banned. Libya had a functioning railroad until 1965, when it was dismantled. In the 1990s the Libyan government began to build two railroad lines: one that would run from the Tunisian border to Tripoli and Mistratah, then stretch south to the desert town of Sabha, where iron ore is mined, and the other slated to link the Egyptian border to the coastal town of Tobruk. Although they were planned for completion in 1994, both lines are not yet finished, although an Egyptian and a Spanish company have been hired to supply parts. All construction on these railroads has ceased as a result of the war.

MODERN LIVING

For years posters have proclaimed "a house for all" or "a car for all." This dream is fast approaching reality for many urbanites, although the house may be no more than an apartment in a hastily constructed building.

However, many Libyans now think there is little point in working toward personal wealth when there is no stability in the country. The society that was created by Gaddafi's high ideals is riddled with incompetence, corruption,

The Kingdom of Italy constructed nearly 248.5 miles (400 km) of railway lines in Libya. The last line the Italians started to create was the Tripoli-Benghazi line in summer 1941, but their defeat in World War II stopped construction at the beginning.

and apathy. Few officials on the hundreds of committees are willing to take responsibility for decisions, as many have been arrested for "failing" the new society. Part of the reason for the uprising was disillusionment with the Gaddafi government and leadership.

In May 1980 a new currency was introduced. Anyone possessing more than $2,100 worth of the old currency received no more than a receipt for the excess. All wealth has been collected by the state, to be redistributed when necessary. Many Libyans were found to have been hiding money in their houses.

Since the UN sanctions were suspended in 1999, numerous foreign development projects have improved the quality of life in the country. Most Libyans have access to proper sewage, water, electricity and telephone services. Water remains scarce, and a purification plant has been opened in Tobruk. Construction has begun on a huge desalination plant near Tripoli to purify seawater. However, in view of the escalating debts owed to foreign contractors, it seems unlikely that anything other than essential projects will be completed.

In 2000 the Italian government funded a center for agricultural experimentation in an effort to make Libya self-sufficient in food production. Still the majority of foreign investment that has returned to Libya in recent years centers on improved access to oil and petroleum facilities.

MIGRANT WORKERS

An estimated 20.74 percent of Libyan citizens were unemployed, and about one-third lived below the national poverty line when the uprising began in 2011. More than 16 percent of families had none of their members earning a stable income, while 43.3 percent of the families in Libya had just one member earning a stable income. Despite one of the highest unemployment rates in the region, there was a consistent labor shortage, with more than a million migrant workers present on the market. These migrant workers formed the bulk of the refugees leaving Libya after the beginning of hostilities.

THE NEW ECONOMY

With the bloody and dark days of the civil war behind them, it is hoped that Libya's economy will be able to grow and develop. Under Gaddafi, the country's economy has been dominated by oil and it is estimated that oil generated about 80 percent of Gaddafi's regime's revenue. Little of the revenue generated trickled down to ordinary Libyans and it is hoped that the country's oil industry will be able to provide the revenue that will help other sectors to grow.

Gaddafi's iron grip on the industry, as well a corrupt government stifled the growth of other sectors. Now that the country has been given a rare fresh start, it is hoped that the economy will be able to diversify and that with a more stable foundation, private businesses and enterprises will be encouraged to grow and thrive. Sectors such as agriculture, tourism, and financial services have been earmarked as areas of potential growth.

In response to the civil war, the UN security council and other governments such as the U.S. and Britain froze an estimated $150 billion of Libyan assets. With the death of Gadaffi, the UN, U.S., Britain and other counties have lifted sanctions on the Libyan central bank, freeing up much needed finances. The cash flow will go toward paying salaries as well as restoring key services in the country.

INTERNET LINKS

http://globaledge.msu.edu/countries/libya/economy/

This site provides a concise summary of Libya's economy before the outbreak of the civil war.

http://rt.com/news/economy-oil-gold-libya/

This is an interesting article, complete with a video clip, postulating the theory that intervention in Libya by Western powers was to stop Colonel Gaddafi from introducing a single African currency.

"The agricultural revolution will enable the Libyan people to earn their living, to eat freely the food that was normally imported from overseas—this is freedom, this is independence, and this is the revolution."
—Muammar Gaddafi, on the Great Man-Made River Project

ENVIRONMENT

The beautiful coastline along Cyrenaica.

5

LIBYA IS MOSTLY DESERT, A difficulty for a nation that wants to produce enough food to feed its people. Gaddafi's dream was of a self-sufficient Libya in terms of agricultural production and industry and trade as well.

When Gaddafi came to power in 1969, the country underwent intensive industrialization—when the government could pay for it. Projects such as the Great Man-Made River transformed the topography of the North African country but with serious consequences for the natural environment.

Some of the most arid areas of the Sahara Desert are found in Libya, where no animals or vegetation can survive. Droughts occur

Rock formations around the Akakus Mountains.

Environmental issues in Libya include desertification and very limited natural freshwater resources.

Gaberoun Lake. The growing Libyan population has placed a great strain on its limited water supply.

frequently and sometimes last as long as two years. It is no surprise that the country's main environmental issues revolve around water: its sources, its distribution, and its purity. Traditionally Bedouin herders relied on regional wells and oases, but population pressures now place so much strain on the desert ecosystem that alternative sources of water must be found.

Libya's drive toward development does not always take into account the environmental consequences of rapid industrialization. Although the country has signed many international agreements, including those on desertification, climate change, marine dumping, and hazardous waste, progress does not always take into account the long-term effects of the new projects. Many generations later, Libyans may find that what initially brought them prosperity has in fact made things worse.

WATER

In a desert country brimming with oil wells and petroleum resources, water is a scarce commodity. On the coast, desalination plants remove dissolved

Libyans splashing in the waters of the Gurdabiya Dam, part of the Great Man-Made River.

minerals (mostly salt and other sediments) from Mediterranean seawater, but the process is expensive. It costs several dollars to produce 35.3 cubic feet (1 cubic m) of desalinated water. In addition desalination plants are extremely inefficient and extract only 15 to 50 percent fresh water from seawater.

In the 1960s a team searching for oil fields deep underground discovered a vast sea of aquifers under Libya's southern desert. Aquifers are great pools of fresh water trapped beneath layers of rock. Libya's southern aquifers were formed many thousands of years ago, when the Mediterranean Sea reached all the way to the Tibesti Mountains near Libya's border with Chad. Geological activity created the ranges of the Green Mountains, and basins were formed under the rocks beneath them. From 38,000 to 10,000 years ago, Libya had ample rainfall, and over the millennia, water gradually seeped through sedimentary rock to collect in the underground pools. The aquifers, undisturbed for ages, are now being drained to provide fresh water for Libya's cities and farms. About three-quarters of the Libyan population depend on water that is piped in from the Nubian Sandstone Aquifer System. The pipe through which most of the water is channeled is known as the Great Man-Made River.

DESERT SPECIES

Most people mistakenly think that the desert consists only of sand and rocks. The Sahara Desert, of which Libya is a part, has varied ecosystems of plant, animal, and insect life. Small plants germinate quickly after the rains, and fields of colorful flowers carpet the desert for days or weeks afterward. The plants must grow and reproduce quickly under the desert sun to escape dehydration and death. Still seeds can lie buried under the Saharan sands for up to a decade until there is enough rain for growth, when once again the desert blooms.

Although the Libyan Desert is one of the hottest and driest areas of the Sahara, reptiles and insects have adapted well to the challenges of survival. Lizards and desert snakes burrow under the ground during the day to escape the hot desert sun but come out to bask in the gentle warmth of morning and evening. Scorpions burrow deep into the sand and impart a dangerous and sometimes lethal sting to anyone who unwittingly steps in their path. Around the desert oases there are mosquitoes, which breed in any stagnant water they can find and plague the population, even in one of the driest and most remote areas of the world.

Because of increased development and population pressure, the mammals of Libya face increased danger and many species are in decline. The famous Barbary lion of North Africa, used in bloody games at the Colosseum during the days of the Roman Empire, is now found only in special breeding areas. In the early 20th century it was hunted almost to extinction. Now there are none left in the wild. City people increasingly hunt the ibex, a small gazelle perfectly adapted to rocky and dry terrain, and they are quickly becoming an endangered species. Unfortunately Libyans are not aware of the pressures they are placing on their environment or the plight of endangered animals that live within their borders. Many international organizations, such as the African Conservation Foundation and the World Wildlife Fund, are starting programs to save the desert species.

THE PRESSURES OF AGRICULTURE

With water so scarce, it is surprising that Libya can produce even a quarter of its food needs. In recent decades, many local aquifers have dried up and filled with salt water from the sea. Water tainted with salt and high in minerals kills crops and contaminates the entire aquifer.

Under the North African sun, evaporation rates are high. Half of all water used for irrigation is lost under the sun's burning rays. Traditional farming methods are inefficient, and much water is wasted during transportation or watering. To keep their land productive, Libyan farmers use 1,627 short tons (1,476 metric tons) of fertilizer per square mile (570,000 kilograms per square km) of land—the 23rd-highest use of fertilizer in the world. In 2003 Libya signed an agreement with the UN Food and Agricultural Organization (FAO) for more than $21 million of agricultural aid, which will modernize and improve seed production in the country.

Food accounts for 20 percent of Libya's imports. This creates dependence on the outside world. Libya hopes to not only become self-sufficient but also to return to being the bread basket of North Africa, a position it held in antiquity. That might not be realistic, because climatic changes over the last 4,000 years have resulted in a steady increase in deserts.

THE GROWING DESERT

Ten thousand years ago the deserts of Libya were green and lush with rolling plains and abundant wildlife. What is now the Sahara Desert even sported tropical rain forest high in the mountains. Scientists believe that 8,000 years ago, the Earth rotated slightly on its axis, with devastating results. The plains that had been fertile dried up and the desert rapidly claimed what had once been productive farmland. To this day the process continues and desertification is a serious problem in Libya. Already 95 percent of the country is desert and agricultural land is of poor quality.

The deserts and their borders are very fragile ecosystems. Any change in rainfall has a dramatic effect on vegetation. Desertification occurs when the

The coast at Tripoli.

area that borders a desert, called a transition zone, comes under pressure from increasing human population. Herds of livestock trample the plant life and harden the soil so it is more vulnerable to wind and rain erosion. Overgrazing destroys what is left. Firewood collection eventually destroys the trees. The deserts of Libya thus look destined for expansion.

THE FRAGILE SEA

Since the days of the early Phoenician settlers, life in Libya has revolved around the Mediterranean coast. Most oceans and seas filter waste and debris efficiently, although man-made pollutants, such as plastics and metals, are becoming an increasing problem.

The Mediterranean Sea is one of the most polluted bodies of water in the world. It is unable to renew itself because of its enclosed shape, which restricts water circulation and flushing. The sewage, plastic waste, oil runoffs, and chemical pollutants that are dumped in its waters daily cause increasing damage to the sea's fragile ecosystem. Libya has signed international agreements concerning marine dumping and wetlands preservation in an effort to protect its 1,100-mile (1,770-km) coastline from environmental pollution and contamination.

Of all the pollutants that threaten the Mediterranean Sea, oil causes the most permanent damage. Since 1983 it has been illegal to dump oil in the Mediterranean, but tankers traveling between the Black Sea, southern Europe, North Africa, and the Middle East continue to release excess oil residues. Experts estimate that up to 363,763 short tons (330,000 metric tons) of oil are illegally dumped in the Mediterranean each year. Petroleum has many carcinogenic substances, and oil dumping causes immense damage to the tourism and fishing industries.

For centuries the people of the Mediterranean coast have depended on the sea for survival. Libyan fishermen catch about 35,770 short tons (32,450 metric tons) of fish in the Mediterranean Sea each year, but fish populations are declining due to the high oil residue in coastal waters. Modern fishing methods such as netting have resulted in over-fishing in most areas and the marine populations are not given a chance to replenish their previously staggering numbers. Issues such as the dumping of open sewage and the harvesting of red coral for tourist curios have contributed to the decline of marine life in the Mediterranean. In recent years awareness of the sea's pollution has grown and the international community is taking action to protect its fragile waterways. The combined impact of sewage, oil byproducts, and industrial waste threatens the nation's coast and the Mediterranean Sea generally. Only about 68 percent of the people living in rural areas have pure drinking water.

INTERNET LINKS

www.anglo-libyan.com/2006/12/libyas-endangered-animals.html

This website contains captivating shots and descriptions of Libya's endangered wildlife.

www.temehu.com/Wild-life-in-sahara.htm

This site includes beautiful shots and descriptions of plants and animals in the Libyan Desert.

www.time.com/time/photogallery/0,29307,2053369,00.html

This is a photo essay on the conflict in Libya. The way the environment is being decimated comes through with every single picture.

LIBYANS

A Libyan girl dressed up for celebrations at Medina.

6

ALMOST ALL LIBYANS TODAY ARE Arabic-speaking Muslims, descended from the Arabs who settled in the area during the last 1,200 years. Many of the early Arabs married into Berber families or into the families of the descendants of Roman or Greek colonists, and so few Libyans today are of pure Arab descent. Some Libyans look like Turks or Egyptians, while others have the darker skin of the desert nomads.

Although the desert-separated areas of Tripolitania, Cyrenaica, and Fezzan have been one country since 1951, Libyans still tend to think tribally as well as nationally. The tribe is the basic unit of Libya's social structure and the *bayt* (bait)—the family within the tribe—is the social group to which they feel they belong.

MINORITY GROUPS

In the southern oases, there are a few communities of pure Berber ancestry. Proud of their origins, they tend to live apart from other Libyans. There are some Libyans who think of themselves as Turkish, or descendants of Turkish soldiers who settled in the area in the days of the Ottoman Empire.

A Libyan mother with her child.

Another minority group is the Sharifs, who live only in Fezzan oases and claim descent from the Prophet Muhammad. There are black Africans from Sudan and countries south of the Sahara, many of whom were originally brought to Libya as slaves. Most are now Muslims and are considered Libyans.

A few Maltese sponge fishers live on the coast. There were once small colonies of Italian farmers, who settled in Libya during the Italian occupation, but they were expelled in 1970.

AFRICAN ARABS

Some say that Arabs form as much as 97 percent of Libya's population, or more than 6.4 million people, and that two-thirds of all Arabs in the world live in Africa.

Most of Libya's population is crowded in the north near the Mediterranean coast where there is a greater chance for employment. More than 95 percent of Libyans live in Tripolitania and Cyrenaica, where they have a better quality of life and good access to government services. Fewer than 5 percent of Libyans live in Fezzan, mostly Bedouin and other groups that can survive in the harsh desert region. On the Mediterranean coastal strip, Libyans are exposed to a modern lifestyle, Western ideas, and contact with foreign workers, but they are still strongly influenced by traditional Islamic customs.

Many Libyan families have been farmers for generations, although few produce more than just enough for their own small community to live on.

In the cities of Tripoli and Benghazi, one can see the sharp contrast between rich and poor, despite Gaddafi's claims of equal distribution of wealth. Senior army officers, administrators, directors of state companies, lawyers, and foreign technical experts all live in newly built suburbs where shops sell black-market goods from abroad.

The bulk of the people live in state-built apartment buildings that are short on space, light, and hygiene. They line up for food at the state-controlled supermarkets. On the outskirts of the cities are the spreading shanty towns.

THE BEDOUIN

Deep in the Libyan Desert, there is a semi-nomadic group of people called the Bedouin. Their name means "desert dwellers" in Arabic. Their territory stretches from the vast deserts of North Africa to the rocky sands of the Middle East. Although they are divided into separate groups with their own territory, the Bedouin share a common culture of herding camels and goats. They measure their wealth by the number of animals in their herd and the quality of their thoroughbred Arabian horses. Bedouins live in family groups called clans and have to move their camps several times a year to find fresh grazing lands for their herds.

Traditionally the term *Bedouin* refers to camel-raising tribes, but due to economic changes, many are now settled or raising sheep.

Bedouin men sitting next to their makeshift dwelling on the Mesak Settafek Plateau.

For centuries the Bedouin have been known for their hospitality and courage. During medieval times they often raided caravans and desert outposts for gold and other booty. During the Islamic Empire rulers found the Bedouin impossible to control and often let them rule themselves. Even today the Bedouin enjoy a semi-autonomous existence in Libya.

Despite the Libyan government's attempts to organize the Bedouin, most prefer their traditional way of life in the desert. Even young Bedouin men who work in the cities return frequently to their camps in times of trial and celebration, and their roots remain strong.

THE BERBERS

When the Arab invaders swept across North Africa in the seventh century, the fiercest resistance came from the northwest (now Tunisia, Algeria, and Morocco). The Arabs called the area Jazirat Al Maghreb, or "the island of the west." The inhabitants of the area were Berbers, and their descendants still live in Libya. They are believed to be the original inhabitants of North Africa.

A fortified Berber granary built in the 12th century. Berber families would store their produce such as grains and olive oil in the granary for safekeeping.

A Berber man making tea. The nomadic desert people are known for their hospitality.

It is thought that the Berbers, also known as the Amazigh (meaning "free men"), once inhabited the entire northern half of the African continent. After the Arab invasion many Berbers converted to Islam. From the 11th to the 13th centuries, two Berber groups called the Almoravids and Almohads became powerful enough to build Islamic empires in northwestern Africa and Spain.

Now making up little more than 3 percent of the Libyan population, pure-blooded Berbers live in inaccessible mountain areas such as Jabal Nafusah and a few isolated oases in Fezzan where their ancestors retreated to escape the Arabs. They grow crops and keep herds of sheep and goats, often living a semi nomadic life to find sufficient pasture.

This distinct culture, suppressed and oppressed by the Libyan regime, has risen to new prominence in the course of the 2011 Libyan civil war, when their initiatives led to the Nafusa Mountains becoming a major front in the war. The terrain and topography of the region are critical strategic factors, constraining mechanized advances from the flat plain and plateau, and favoring guerrilla tactics based on close local knowledge and the advantage of high ground. However, the unveiling of the new Libyan cabinet left the

A Tuareg man. Most Tuaregs live around oases in the desert.

minority Amazighs unrepresented. Angered, hundreds of Amazighs took to the streets to protest their exclusion, demanding an apology from Libya's interim premier.

Berbers consider themselves members of individual groups rather than a single nation. Most are Muslim and belong to the Kharijite sect of Islam. They revere local saints and holy places from their religious tradition.

The old Berber language and their reluctance to marry out of their group set them apart from other ethnic groups.

Berber women enjoy more personal freedom than Arab women. They had the right to own property, get a divorce, and remarry long before Muslim women gained such rights.

PEOPLE OF THE BLUE VEIL

The Tuareg are a fiercely independent desert people who do not consider themselves as belonging to any particular country. The remaining Tuareg groups are found in Libya, northwestern Niger, and Mali. Many are still nomadic, but their ancient way of life is now restricted by national borders, so most have settled around oases.

The Tuareg can be distinguished from the white-clothed Berbers by their black or dark blue cloaks and are known as the People of the Blue Veil. The origin of the custom of wearing a veil grew from the need for protection from sand and sun, but it is also a mark of pride. In contrast to Islamic tradition, it is the Tuareg man who veils his face; the woman is not so bound, though she will usually cover her mouth in the presence of strangers or her father-in-law. Property is inherited by children through the mother, not the father.

Like the Bedouin, the Tuareg were notorious for raiding settlements and stealing livestock. The Tuareg once achieved brief Hollywood fame as the "bad guys" in the movie *Beau Geste*. The 2005 film *Sahara* featured a fictionalized

The population of Libya is estimated to be 6.6 million. Life expectancy is 75.34 years for men and 80.08 years for women. Since 1965 access to improved medical care and nutrition has resulted in a decline in the death rate to 3.4 per 1,000 people. The annual growth rate is about 2.1 percent, and the infant mortality rate is 20.09 per 1,000 births. Estimates show that 82.6 percent of Libyans are literate. Libya has the highest literacy rate in northern Africa. Eighty percent of Libyans live in cities.

group of Tuareg as a faction in a civil war under way in Mali. They speak their own language, which they write in their own ancient alphabet. Part of Tuareg society are the black African *iklan* (ik-LAWN), who were originally slaves captured during raids across the Niger.

THE MODERN LIBYAN

Outspoken opposition to Gaddafi's theories of the ideal socialist Arab state were ruthlessly punished under Gaddafi's regime. Many people in the business community were arrested or had their property confiscated under the anti-corruption laws introduced in 1994. The job of confiscating assets was carried out by Purification Committees, which were made up of young military officers and students. It is also believed that hundreds of people were sent to prison for political reasons. The eastern part of the country became impoverished under Gaddafi's economic theories. At the start of the civil war, one-fifth of Libyans were unemployed, and one-third lived below the national poverty line.

IMMIGRANT WORKERS

Libya's history of colonization and invasions has made Libyans suspicious of foreigners. Foreigners have at various times been banned from working in Libya. During the UN sanctions (1992—99), Gaddafi ordered nearly all Americans and Europeans to leave the country, but after 1999 European companies were once again encouraged to invest in Libya. The suspension of sanctions by the United Nations in 1999 produced an increase in the number of foreigners working in Libya. They are valued for their expertise in technical fields, as few Libyans have such expertise. The foreigners include Italians, Germans, Britons, Thais, Koreans, and Indians.

WHAT TO WEAR?

For centuries style and clothing throughout the Middle East and across Africa were dictated by Islamic tradition. Men wore long white robes that kept them cool during the day. They also wore a rope-bound head scarf or wound turban. The way the turban was knotted was a clear indication of the

A group of Libyan men dressed in the long, flowing robes of Islamic tradition.

area in which one lived. Women also wore robes to preserve their modesty, an important virtue in Islamic society. From the age of puberty, they kept their faces veiled whenever men were present, and married women often wore black to denote their marital status.

Gradually the styles of the West arrived. The red Turkish fez and European suits spread through the Mediterranean Arab world and to Libya. Apart from the Arabic posters, shop names, and road signs, there is little difference between the streets of Tripoli or Benghazi and those in almost any Mediterranean port. Girls wear bright-colored dresses, often with dark-colored trousers beneath for modesty; boys wear shirts and jeans.

College students and young married couples tend to wear modern clothes: an open-necked shirt in summer, a turtleneck in winter, with a leather jacket or zipped parka for men. Women still wear a head scarf, even with a blouse and skirt.

Traditional dresses are long and flowing, and worn with charms and necklaces that are believed to protect the wearer from evil spells. Koranic verses are also worn around the neck. Army uniforms are visible, as are modern suits with shirt and tie and traditional Arab robes for older people. Young men go bareheaded; others wear a black or white Islamic cap.

South of the coastal cities, people wear the Arab robes of Islamic tradition. The robes are white, loose, and flowing, and are more comfortable to wear in the hot desert climate because they trap the wind and reflect the sunlight.

INTERNET LINKS

www.ewpnet.com/libya/customs.htm
This site contains interesting pictures of the Libyan dress code.

www.temehu.com/Libyan-People.htm
This site provides a comprehensive look at the different groups of people that live in Libya.

LIFESTYLE

A street at Bab al-Menchia in Tripoli.

7

WEALTH FROM THE OIL INDUSTRY brought social challenges as the income gap between the rich and poor widened dramatically. However, one thing that did not change was religion. Islam remains central to Libya's way of life. Before the revolution, Gaddafi enforced an even stricter interpretation of the Islamic code.

Islamic life is bound by tradition. Families in Libya dress mainly in traditional clothes. They attend the mosque regularly, and each day is structured around the five prayer times. People stay close to home in the evening. No one goes out for a drink. Alcohol is forbidden, and there are no bars or nightclubs. Even the innumerable cafés, selling cups of sweet, strong coffee and local fizzy drinks, are threatened by a shortage of basic food products.

Friday is the Islamic holy day, as Saturday is for Jews and Sunday for Christians. Muslims go to the mosque at noon on Fridays to join in public prayer and on other days if time permits.

However, the Libyan way of life in urban areas along the coast is modern and liberal when compared to the centuries-old lifestyle inland. Working in the fields or tending the animals is considered a reward in itself. People in those areas have been forced to live that way not because of religion but because of the environment.

The popular uprising that erupted in February 2011, and the subsequent battles between rebels and pro-Gadaffi forces, brought to the fore the frustrations of ordinary Libyans demanding a better life. Those fighting Gadaffi said they wanted freedom, but they also wanted economic opportunities that have long been elusive because of rampant patronage and nepotism.

HOMES

A traditional house in the old town of Ghadames.

The traditional home of a prosperous Libyan family is built to an accepted pattern. Behind a stout wooden door is a corridor leading to a bright patio. The rooms of the house are grouped around this open-air square, which often has a pool or fountain in the middle. The square is the focal point for family activities. The rooms have plain, whitewashed walls, but the floors are decorated with carpets and tasseled cushions on low benches. Some houses also have intricately designed tiles and ceilings.

The days of such lavish styles, which go back to the days of the Umayyad Empire in the eighth century, are passing. Most city-dwellers live in apartment buildings. Color-washed walls are cheaper than Persian carpets, though families like to have rugs if they can afford them. A low couch along one wall is common, and embroidered cushions take the place of armchairs. The kitchen area is traditionally the woman's private domain.

Farther inland many houses are built of mud bricks. Mud walls are perfectly suited to the desert climate because they keep the house cool during summer and trap warm air during the coldest months of winter.

Most houses have only one floor, with a flat roof and sometimes molded pinnacles on each corner. They have very small windows—partly for privacy and partly because the walls are stronger that way. Fancier homes in the cities are built around a central courtyard. Narrow alleyways between the houses provide shade.

A WOMAN'S LIFE

Islamic society is patriarchal—families are headed by the father figure. For years in Libya, only boys went to school. No one could see any point in educating girls, who were expected to become wives and mothers.

In Libya women have had the right to vote and run for public office since 1963, but few choose to do so. Gaddafi tried to change the inferior status of women by passing legislation that gives them equal rights. They have access to education and employment, but most choose jobs dominated by women such as nursing, teaching, social work, and secretarial work. Islamic law in Libya denies women custody of children, alimony payments, and equal inheritance after divorce.

It is very important in Libyan society for women to be modest. Only a woman's hands, feet, and face may be left uncovered in public, and to disregard these conventions is a serious offence against family honor. Within an Arab group, a man's reputation depends largely on the behavior of the women in his family. Most girls start wearing the traditional black cloak and veil at puberty, but in some families even six-year-old girls cover their heads.

Many Libyan women work outside the home. Raising children and taking care of the house remain women's responsibilities, however, and most women in Libya stay home at least when their children are very young. More traditional families restrict a woman's outdoor movements to only the most essential activities. Before the revolution, working mothers enjoyed a range of benefits designed to encourage them to continue working even after marriage and childbirth, including cash bonuses for the first child and free daycare centers. A woman could retire at the age of 55 years, and she was entitled to a pension. The revolution launched in February 2011 has turned life in Libya upside-down. Retail sales have dropped amid the uncertainty, and some shop owners in battle-scarred towns don't even bother to roll up their metal store shutters in the morning. The Libyan dinar is depreciating, with $1 trading at 1.85 dinars on the black market, compared with the official 1.2-dinar-per-dollar exchange rate.

Women in Libya are able to enjoy the right to vote and access to education.

HEALTH

A doctor stands in an operating room at a hospital in Sirte. Many medical facilities were severely damaged during the civil war.

Gaddafi's socialist government instituted free health services and increased facilities dramatically. In comparison to other states in the Middle East, the health status of the population is relatively good. Childhood immunization is almost universal. Clean water supply has increased and sanitation has been improved.

There are two large hospitals, in Tripoli and Benghazi, and many smaller hospitals and clinics around the country, while mobile health units visit the country districts. However, many of these facilities have been damaged by the civil war.

Some schools provide health services and supplement the children's diet, and there were some mother-and-child care centers. Instead of the Red Cross, there are clinics run by the Red Crescent Society as it is called in Islamic countries.

In the years following the revolution from 1969 to 1978, the number of doctors in Libya increased four- to five-fold. The number of medical doctors and dentists reportedly increased sevenfold between 1970 and 1985, producing a ratio of one doctor per 673 citizens. In 1985 about one-third of the doctors in the Libya were native-born, with the remainder being primarily expatriate foreigners. Traditions that prevent married women from coming into contact with any man other than their husband have made it hard for Libyan women to be trained as nurses or doctors.

Malaria has been wiped out with the aid of the World Health Organization, and significant progress was made against trachoma (an eye disease that can lead to blindness) and leprosy. However, a drug-resistant strain of tuberculosis has emerged.

DEATH AND BURIAL

Libyan children are brought up not to be frightened by the idea of death. Muslims believe that everything comes from God and, however difficult the circumstances may be, everything happens for the best. It is considered holy to face life's trials calmly and without complaint. Certainly the Bedouin meet death all too often in the harsh desert.

No Libyan family would ever put an elderly relative into an old-age home. They are glad to have elderly family members at home, where they can turn to them for advice. With their family around them, the elderly accept the approach of death in a dignified manner. A Libyan might well gather friends and relatives and say farewell to each one before he or she dies.

According to tradition, the dead body is washed in water or sand. It is then clothed in fresh linen and buried in a shallow grave. The custom is to lay the corpse facing Mecca. In the desert few people attend this ceremony. In the towns, many do, anxious to help carry the body. Women are not allowed to be part of the funeral procession because it is believed that they are too emotional. Exaggerated expressions of grief are not allowed in Islam. For ordinary people, no monuments or headstones are used. Muslims believe that once a person is dead, the body is of no further use.

INTERNET LINKS

http://lallalydia.blogspot.com/2007/12/modern-day-amazons-colonel-qaddafis.html

This is an interesting article on Gaddafi's gorgeous female bodyguards, complete with pictures.

http://lcweb2.loc.gov/frd/cs/profiles/Libya.pdf

This site includes a detailed report on life in Libya.

www.icrc.org/eng/resources/documents/update/2011/libya-update-2011-07-05.htm

This site provides an update on what the Red Crescent is doing to assist in Libya.

RELIGION

Libyan Muslims at the Mawlay Mohamed Mosque for Friday prayers.

8

T O UNDERSTAND THE PEOPLE OF Libya, one must understand their religion, because religion governs their lives, their education, their language, and their hopes for the future.

LIBYA AND SUNNI ISLAM

The religion of Libya is Islam. The word *Islam* means "submission to the will of Allah." *Allah* is the word Muslims use for God, who is considered compassionate and merciful but cannot be fully known. Islam is divided into two sects: About 90 percent of the total Muslim population are members of the Sunni sect; the rest belong to the Shi'ite sect. Most Libyans are Sunni Muslims.

The interior of the Gurgi Mosque that was built in 1833.

Most Libyans adhere to the Sunni branch of Islam, which provides both a spiritual guide for individuals and a keystone for government policy. Its tenets stress a unity of religion and state rather than a separation or distinction between the two, and even those Muslims who have ceased to believe fully in Islam retain Islamic habits and attitudes.

The ancient town of Medina. The Prophet Muhammad is buried here.

Islam is a practical religion with clear rules for living and worship. Africa has historical and political ties to the Middle East, where Islam continues to be the dominant religion. About 20 percent of the world's billion Muslims are found in Africa.

Since the 1969 revolution, everything Arabic and Islamic in Libya has been intensified, while anything considered contrary to Islamic beliefs is destroyed or forbidden. Gaddafi strongly encouraged conversions to Islam in African countries such as Nigeria.

THE PROPHET MUHAMMAD

The Prophet Muhammad, the founder of Islam, was born in Mecca, a prosperous trading town in what is now Saudi Arabia, in A.D. 570, more than five centuries after the birth of Jesus Christ. After the Prophet Muhammad's father died, his mother could not afford to look after him, so he was sent to live with his grandfather in the desert. He started as a herd boy and later worked for his uncle, traveling with the camel caravans.

At the age of 25, he married a woman named Khadija, who became one of his staunchest supporters. They had six children, but the Prophet Muhammad's surviving descendants were all the children of his daughter, Fatimah.

As the Prophet Muhammad traveled, he became aware of Judaism and Christianity. He also knew that many people in Arabia still worshiped idols. He traveled into the mountains, where he began to have dreams and visions. Muslims believe that while he was in the mountains, the Prophet Muhammad heard the words of God spoken to him by the angel Gabriel. Although the Prophet Muhammad himself could not read or write, he told others what he had heard. The words were written down and became the holy book of Islam, the Koran.

When the Prophet Muhammad took his words to Mecca in the hope that people there would turn to Allah, he met with fierce opposition. In A.D. 622, preceded by about 70 men and their families, he migrated to a town farther north called Medina, where the people welcomed his arrival. There, he built the first mosque.

By A.D. 629, after years of fierce fighting between the two towns, the Prophet Muhammad's support was strong enough for him to lead his forces into Mecca. The square enclosure that had once housed idols became the sacred *Ka'bah* (kah-AH-bah), the central shrine of pilgrimage for Muslims.

The Prophet Muhammad died in A.D. 632 and was buried at Medina. Muslims do not worship the Prophet Muhammad, but he is respected and honored as God's last prophet.

The Merciful, the Compassionate, the Forgiver, the Forgiving, the Clement, the Generous, the Affectionate, the Kind . . .
—some of the 99 names Muslims have for God

THE FIVE PILLARS OF ISLAM

Every true Muslim accepts five basic religious duties:

1. *Shahada* (sha-HAD-ah)—the confession of faith. This means to bear witness that there is no god other than Allah and that the Prophet Muhammad is his final messenger and prophet.
2. *Salat* (sahl-AHT)—prayer. This means to pray five times daily, facing the direction of Mecca, at daybreak, noon, mid-afternoon, after sunset, and early in the night.
3. *Zakat* (za-KAHT)—alms giving. This refers to giving 2.5 percent of one's annual earnings to the poor and needy.
4. Fasting during the month of Ramadan (rah-mah-DAHN). Muslims go without food or drink between dawn and sunset for the 30 days of the lunar month.
5. *Hajj*—pilgrimage. This refers to making the pilgrimage to Mecca once in a lifetime.

Muslims also have six main beliefs as the foundation of their faith. They believe that Allah is the only God and that there exist angels, holy books, prophets, the Day of Judgment, and pre-destiny.

SHI'ISM

Shi'ites make up the second-largest Islamic sect in Libya. Shi'a Muslims broke away from the dominant Sunnis for reasons of theology and politics. One difference stems from arguments over the Prophet Muhammad's successors as caliphs, the spiritual leaders of Muslims. The Shi'ites wanted the caliphate to descend through Ali, the Prophet Muhammad's son-in-law. Ali eventually became the fourth caliph, but he was murdered soon after. Since then the Shi'ites have accused the later caliphs, whom the Sunnis followed, of being usurpers.

Shi'ites also regard their holy men as having far greater authority than ordinary Muslims. This opposes the Sunni belief that their religious leaders are ordinary Muslims who have received extra training as teachers and leaders in prayer.

The Ghadames New Mosque is a modern contrast to the ancient town of Ghadames in which it is found.

PLACE OF PRAYER

A mosque is a place of worship, as is a church. Indeed many buildings have been used as one and then the other. Structurally the greatest difference is that a Christian worshiper usually enters a church at one end of the building to see the altar at the far end, whereas a Muslim more often enters the mosque in the middle of one of the long walls and faces across.

Although churches were traditionally built with the altar at the eastern end (for most of Europe, the eastern end pointed to Jerusalem, where Jesus was crucified and resurrected), mosques are oriented so that worshipers directly face Mecca, the sacred city of Islam.

Every mosque needs a tower from which the muezzin, or mosque official, can give the call to prayer. Often the towers are in the shape of a slender minaret, with hundreds of steps leading to the top. Today a muezzin usually uses a loudspeaker system, made essential by the clamor of the modern city. The muezzin was once chosen from among the blind, so that they could concentrate on the prayer and not be distracted by the view from the top of the minaret.

A running fountain in the courtyard is also an essential facility for worshipers, because Islam prescribes that people cleanse themselves with water before they pray. Some mosques even have a bathhouse, similar to a Turkish bath, attached.

WITHIN THE BUILDING

To people who are used to ornate, furnished Christian churches, a mosque may seem empty. Whether large or small, the mosque is essentially an open space covered with carpets for the kneeling worshipers.

There are only two particular features. In the eastern wall is an empty recess called the *mihrab* (mi-RAHB), which indicates the direction of Mecca. There is also the *minbar* (MIN-bar), or pulpit, often in the shape of a narrow flight of steps, from which the imam leads prayers and preaches.

No images or pictures adorn the walls or pillars because Islam forbids the depiction of living creatures, but mosques are often resplendent with artistic shapes, colorful tiles, geometric designs, and Arabic calligraphy.

The decorated walls, the rich carpets, the stained-glass windows, and the architectural symmetry all combine to contribute to an atmosphere of holy splendor.

PILGRIMAGE TO MECCA

Once a small desert town visited only by caravans of camels, Mecca is now a major city in Saudi Arabia and the holiest place of Islam. It had some importance even before the birth of the Prophet Muhammad. A black stone, probably a meteorite, was said to have been sent by God. The black stone was built into the wall of a square enclosure that housed a profusion of idols. That square building is the Ka'bah. Today it is draped with a ceremonial black cloth

"Say to the believing men that they should lower their gaze and guard their modesty; that will make for greater purity for them; and Allah is well acquainted with all that they do. And say to the believing women that they should lower their gaze and guard their modesty; that they should not display their beauty and ornaments except what (must ordinarily) appear thereof; that they should draw their veils over their bosoms and not display their beauty."
—the Koran

embroidered with gold called the *kiswah* (KEYS-wa). The Great Mosque has been built around the Ka'bah.

Mecca is now an endlessly crowded town among sheltering hills. Muslim pilgrims on their annual pilgrimage are expected to camp in the desert as the Prophet Muhammad once did, but that has not prevented Mecca from becoming a town of hotels and souvenir shops. Traffic is an increasing problem, and there are plans to build elevated bypass roads. Visitors arrive by air or through the adjoining port of Jiddah on the Red Sea.

SUPERSTITIONS

Islamic tradition frowns on superstition. Nevertheless Muslims pay great attention to dreams, which they believe are sent by God. In many communities there are people known for their ability to interpret dreams. Most Libyans believe that dreams have an opposite result. For example, a frightening dream may well be a good sign. Dreams can also be warnings of dire happenings, although such events cannot be avoided—they are "the will of Allah."

Muslims believe that sickness may be sent by God, or through the power of a curse from someone wishing another harm. Many Libyans wear charms, usually a small container with a verse from the Koran, on a leather thong. Some pregnant women wear an earring in the shape of a blue hand with an eye on its palm. The hand is called the *khamsa* (KHAHM-sa), or the hand of Fatimah, and is meant to protect the wearer from harm and bad luck.

Some older Libyans believe in the existence of evil spirits called jinn that live in haunted places. They can drive a person insane or kill them. Jinn are believed to be able to assume the form of snakes, dogs, cats, monsters, or people.

THE HAJJ

Every year, about 3 million Muslims, including many Libyans, make the pilgrimage to Mecca in Saudi Arabia. To make this journey is an honor, a blessing, and the greatest longing of any Muslim.

GENIES AND SPELLS

Strict Muslims like to hear stories from the Koran and about the life of the Prophet Muhammad. Many Libyans also enjoy listening to folktales passed down for many generations that tell of enchanted lands and the spirit world. Many of the fables have a hero who encounters a genie or another type of magical creature that helps him win his fortune. The hero also often meets mythical creatures such as winged birds and fierce monsters, and wicked sorcerers who cast evil spells. Although such stories are frowned upon by strict Islamic tradition, they are very popular with Libyans.

Enormous camps surround Mecca at the time of the pilgrimage. Everyone wears similar clothing, so there is no distinction between rich and poor. Men wear two pieces of seamless white cloth, one wrapped around the lower body, the other draped over the shoulder. Women wear green underclothes and a cloak and veil.

The first task, immediately after arrival in Mecca, is to walk around the walls of the Great Mosque. Then the pilgrims join the throng inside the mosque to walk seven times around the Ka'bah. If possible, they kiss the black stone built into its outside wall, said to be a stone on which Abraham once stood. Next comes the visit to drink from the sacred well of Zamzam, where prayers and ceremonials are recited.

On the eighth day, the pilgrims move to the Mount of Mercy, about 13 miles (21 km) from Mecca. There Muhammad once gave a famous sermon. The pilgrims stand or sit in meditation from midday to sunset. The shelter of an umbrella is permitted if the hajj falls during the intense heat of summer. This visit is considered so important that if it is omitted the pilgrimage is considered to have no value.

At sunset they move to Mina, where three stone pillars representing the devil stand. In Muhammad's time, the three pillars belonged to a popular temple for goddess worship that was demolished when he returned with his followers to Mecca.

"He who helps a Muslim in his worldly distress will be rewarded by Allah on the day of judgment."
—the Prophet Muhammad

On the 10th day the end of the hajj is marked by the great Feast of Sacrifice. It is a time for giving alms, for prayers and rejoicing, for sermons in the open air, and for the sacrifice of a lamb, goat, cow, or camel. The feast officially lasts three days, but the celebrations often continue for a full week.

Each pilgrim washes, cuts off ceremonial locks of hair, and puts on new clothes to symbolize the entering of a new life. After that some pilgrims go back to the Ka'bah for a farewell circling. Before leaving Saudi Arabia, the pilgrim may visit Medina, where Muhammad built his first mosque and where he is buried.

The return of the pilgrims is another cause for celebrations. Many Libyans paint their houses with murals of the pilgrimage, and their neighbors come to congratulate them.

FOOD AND FASTING

An essential principle of Islam is submission to God, and a Muslim's diet must also conform to the will of God. In Libya the Islamic diet is strictly observed.

Alcohol is forbidden in any form. It may not be brought into Libya by visitors, whether or not they are Muslim. As in Judaism, pork products are also forbidden, as the pig is not considered a "clean" animal.

Libyans gathering at Martyr's Square in Tripoli to pray, marking the end of Ramadan, the holy month of fasting.

Fasting is also part of the discipline imposed by the faith. The word *breakfast* reminds us that, after a night without food or drink, we break our fast in the morning. All over the Islamic world, Ramadan is the holy month of fasting. No food or water is permitted from sunrise to sunset. The fast is broken after evening prayers are completed, when the family comes together for a large meal. Non-Muslim visitors to Libya are obliged to respect the fast during Ramadan. During the civil war, there was no cease-fire during Ramadan, though some of the forces still observed and kept their fast even though the Koran makes exceptions for soldiers engaged in war.

MINORITY RELIGIONS IN LIBYA

Before the outbreak of war, Christianity was always a minority religion in Libya since the Arab invasions. The largest Christian group in Libya was the Coptic Orthodox church, with a population of more than 60,000. There was one Anglican congregation in Tripoli, made up mostly of African immigrant workers in Tripoli and which belonged to the Egyptian Anglican diocese. Libya had the largest proportion of Buddhists of any North African country, with 0.3 percent of its population identifying itself as Buddhist.

INTERNET LINKS

http://islam101.net/
This is an educational website on Islam.

www.islam.com/introislam.htm
This is a site covering a wide range of topics and issues relating to Islam.

www.washingtonpost.com/blogs/guest-voices/post/how-is-religion-informing-the-rebels-in-libya/2011/04/02/AF8VXmRC_blog.html
This site contains an interesting article on the role of religion in Libya's civil war.

Gaddafi stressed the universal applicability of Islam, but he also reaffirmed the special status assigned by the Prophet Muhammad to Christians. However, he likened them to misguided Muslims who have strayed from the correct path. Furthermore he assumed leadership of a drive to free Africa of Christianity as well as of the colonialism with which it has been associated.

LANGUAGE

A Libyan reading the Koran, which is written in Arabic.

9

THE LANGUAGE THAT ORIGINATED among the Arabs of the Arabian Peninsula is now spoken by some 150 million people around the world, from Morocco to Malaysia. It is the official language of Libya.

ARABIC

Arabic belongs to the Afro-Asiatic family of languages and is further classified as a Semitic language. Semites are people from the Middle East who are believed to have descended from Shem, Noah's eldest son. The Semitic languages are spoken in North Africa and the Middle East. They include Hebrew and Amharic. Modern spoken Arabic has regional differences, but most Arabic-speaking countries use standard Arabic, based on the language of the Koran, in their books and newspapers.

ANCIENT AFRICA

The most ancient language of Libya is the Numidian language of the Berbers that is still spoken in isolated places in Jabal Nafusah. A modified form of this language remains in *tifinagh* (tee-fee-nawkh), the geometrical alphabet used by the Tuareg. Most Libyan Berbers have adopted Arabic.

The Internet played a vital role in the revolution in Libya, allowing diverse rebel groups to coordinate with each other.

GADDAFI AND THE BERBERS

The Berber minority in Libya suffered great oppression and discrimination under Gaddafi's rule. Gaddafi refused to acknowledge the Berbers as a people and culture and used Arabization as a means to achieve nationalism. He was particularly disdainful of their language, Tamazight. Berber towns were renamed and it was considered illegal for children to be given Berber names until 2009. Schools were not allowed to teach the Berber language. Despite being able to speak Berber, many young Berbers had never seen their language in its written form, much less understand it. This oppression and destruction of their language and identity was part of the reason that Berbers were willing to join in the fight against Gaddafi's rule.

Gaddafi's policies heralded the demise of Tamazight, with people fearful of the repercussions of teaching, using, or promoting the language and culture. But the death of Gaddafi has signaled new hope for the Berbers and the continuation of their language and culture. However, it will be difficult to change the mindsets of the predominantly Arab-speaking population. Previous Arab conquest heralded Arabic as the language of God and stigmatized the use of Tamazight. Berber identity has often been overlooked in favor of nationalism, a call for a unified Libya.

A sign written in Arabic script describing the World Heritage Site of Sabratha.

ARABIC WORDS

In the years when Muslim traders sailed to the shores of the Mediterranean, many European languages adopted words from Arabic. Many places in Arab countries have Arabic names beginning with *Al*, meaning "the."

In chess, a game adopted by Christian Europe from the Islamic world, several of the terms we use today come from the Arabic or Persian languages. The word checkmate *comes from* shah mat, *meaning "the king is dead." The castle is also called the* rook, *which comes from the Persian* rukh. *The word* rook *can also mean "chariot;" the castle/rook moves in a similar straight and powerful manner. The bishop in Arabic is called* al-Fil, *"the elephant."*

English words such as *alcohol, almanac, alfalfa, alcove,* and *algebra* come from Arabic. Here are some others: *admiral, coffee, giraffe, caravan, lemon, kebab,* and *marzipan.*

Words with connected meanings in Arabic often contain the same pattern of consonants. For example, *s-l-m* is the root of words such as *salaam* (meaning "peace"), *Islam,* and *Muslim.*

ARABIC AND THE KORAN

Among the earliest teaching of Islam was the necessity for Muslims to be taught to read. Only then could they read the Koran.

Because all Muslims are required to study the Koran, all Muslims must learn Arabic, because the Koran must be read in Arabic. Muslims believe that the Koran would not truly reflect the word of God in any other language. That is why Arabic is the official spoken and written language of Libya. But because there are many specialists from the Western world working in Libya, other languages such as English and Italian are spoken by some.

The word *Allah* is constantly on the lips of Muslims. It is considered polite to refer to Allah often in conversation. "Praise Allah," "By Allah's permission," and "Allah is great" are as common in conversation as "good-bye." Even a simple matter such as agreeing to meet a friend at a certain time will be marked by the phrase "insh-allah," or "if Allah wills it."

Since the revolution, there has been a revival of the Berber language, which Gaddafi had tried to stamp out.

VISUAL BEAUTY

Arabic was originally written in brush strokes, and its letters still look as if they have been painted rather than printed. The early editions of the Koran were handwritten and are beautiful to look at. Calligraphers used to be held in high regard, largely because there was no printing in the Islamic world until the 18th century.

Muslims are forbidden to depict God in pictures, but they love to describe him in picturesque words. So Arabic calligraphy is one of their primary art forms. In the past, because most calligraphers and their readers knew the Koran by heart, beautiful lettering became more important than legibility.

Pages of a 13th-century Koran printed with beautiful calligraphy.

ARABIC NUMERALS

The number system used for centuries by the Christian world was invented by the Romans and is still known as Roman numerals. In this system, different letters stand for numbers. C stands for a hundred and M for a thousand, because they are the first letters of the Latin words *centum* and *mille*. So, for the number two thousand, two hundred, and twenty-two, the Romans wrote MMCCXXII.

How much simpler it is for people today to write 2,222. Although each figure 2 looks the same, it stands for a different amount according to its position in the number. That is because we use Arabic numerals. This number system was introduced to Spain at the end of the 10th century by the Arabs, who probably borrowed the system from India about 200 years earlier.

It took another 500 years for the rest of Europe to accept this new system. Thanks to the Arabs, the European world was introduced to the use of the digit 0. Without this symbol, the invention of decimals would have been impossible.

Interestingly it was Caliph Haroun al-Raschid (made famous in the *Arabian Nights* stories, though he was a very real person) who did much to spread mathematical ideas. He had many old Greek books translated into Arabic, including Euclid's *Elements on Mathematics* in 1482.

Arabs were also skilled astronomers. Astronomical terms such as *zenith* and *nadir* come from Arabic. Arabs knew enough about astronomy and geography to calculate the circumference and diameter of the Earth. After all, it was from "the East" (perhaps Persia and the Arabian Desert) that the Three Wise Men followed the star to Bethlehem to visit the infant Jesus Christ.

SPELLING ARABIC IN ENGLISH

Writing Arabic words with the English alphabet poses constant problems because there are many sounds in Arabic for which our alphabet has no equivalent. Even so famous an Arab name as Muhammad can also be spelled "Mohammed," "Mehmet," and "Mahomet." Yet none of these gives the exact sound of the true Arabic pronunciation.

In this book, the spellings preferred by English-speaking Muslims have been used. There are books in which the word *Muslim* is spelled "Moslem," and *Koran* is "Al-Qur'an."

IN CONVERSATION

Even non-Arabic-speaking Muslims constantly encounter the classical Arabic language in their daily prayers, the reading of the Koran, and in Arabic writings. God is constantly invoked in conversation, and sayings such as "in the name of God," "thanks be to God," and "may God be with you" are constantly on the believer's lips. *Inshallah*, meaning "if God wills it," is used in various situations, from a polite refusal to sealing an agreement. The Koran is written in classical Arabic, an old-fashioned form of the language. Fortunately now Modern Standard Arabic is used in nearly all written and printed material in Arab countries.

Traditional manners require a series of questions, each with its proper answer, when inquiring about another's health and family. Hands are clasped until the ritual questions have been answered. Important conversations are always accompanied by coffee. It would be the height of bad manners to begin a serious discussion before the pot was finished.

The normal Libyan greeting is *Salaam aleikum* ("peace be with you"), to which the correct reply is *Aleikum as-salaam* ("and also with you"). Another normal greeting is *Sabbahakum Allah bi'l-khair* ("Allah give you a good morning"). Among the Tuareg, a normal greeting includes letting one's palm slide gently across the other person's and then pulling the hand back to touch the chest.

In Libya it is extremely rude to criticize someone to his or her face, so when disagreements occur, family and friends are often brought in to mediate. Tradition demands courtesy in public, and family matters are considered strictly private. Women are never discussed in public, especially not by name. Women may discuss the men in their friends' families, but among men, it is considered immodest and vulgar to mention the women in a man's family.

Gestures form a significant part of any good conversation. "No" is often accompanied with a click of the tongue and a toss of the head.

IN THE MEDIA

All forms of public entertainment in Libya were restricted to the accepted agenda prescribed by Islam. Many expressions of Western culture, including some books, films, magazines, posters, and Christian institutions, were forbidden or viewed with disapproval under Gaddafi. Ever since Arabic became the official language in 1969, all street signs, advertisements, and shop names must be written in Arabic. Speaking languages such as English and Italian in public is discouraged.

Radios, television sets, and satellite dishes are easy to purchase in Libya, and most families own one or the other. The state both owns and controls the media, and under Gaddafi's rule, the censors were quick to edit or cut programs that they saw as threatening moral values, demeaning Libya, or glorifying the West. The government ran Libya's two radio stations: the Great Socialist People's Libyan Arab Jamahiriya Radio, which broadcasts in Libya only in Arabic, and the Voice of Africa, an external station that also ran programs in English and French.

When Libya's national television station was launched in 1968, it was the only channel available in the country. With the advent of satellite technology, however, those who could afford it enjoyed wider access to international programming. Stations that broadcast in Arabic, such as the news channel Al-Jazeera and the Egyptian-run NileTV, which even had an Arabic version of *Sesame Street*, remain popular.

The uprising that began in February 2011 saw the emergence of media outlets affiliated with opponents of Colonel Gaddafi. They include radio stations in areas wrested from the regime's control, and Libya TV—a Qatar-based satellite station. The rebels run a number of newspapers and websites.

There were nearly 354,000 Internet users in Libya by June 2010. Web filtering was selective, focusing on political opposition websites. Social media have served as a battleground for supporters and foes of the former regime.

Since the revolution, "The Voice of Free Libya," a rebel radio station, has been set up.

INTERNET LINKS

http://news.nationalpost.com/2011/07/11/ancient-language-renewed-in-libyan-rebellion/
This is an article on the revival of the Berber language after the fall of Gaddafi.

www.guardian.co.uk/world/2011/may/29/libya-english-radio-tribute-fm
This uplifting article talks about the very first English-language radio station set up in Libya after Gaddafi's fall.

ARTS

A copper worker fabricating metal in the copper souk
in Medina.

10

LIBYAN CULTURE IS ALMOST TOTALLY dependent on Islamic arts and traditions. In all visual arts Islam does not allow any representation of living things.

Muslims believe that anything created by God is perfect and that it would be wrong to copy the sublime in an imperfect way, so there can be no human figures in pictures, sculpture, decorations, or designs in mosques. To make a carving or painting of a human being that can be admired would be like making an idol to be worshiped in a mosque. Instead Libyan artists and architects use intricate patterns of geometric designs or flowers. However, outside of mosques, depictions of people are welcomed.

CAVE PAINTINGS

The oldest form of art in Libya is rock paintings. In Fezzan an Italian expedition found a series of rock paintings that are more than 5,000 years old. Some are painted solid red or black, others in a scraped style resembling rock engraving.

Although less spectacular, the rock paintings must have a similar origin to the rock art discovered in Algeria's Tassili N'ajjer, which is located near the Libyan border. The oldest rock paintings depict the Sahara as a green pasture with people hunting elephants, antelopes, and giraffes. The whole history of the Sahara is portrayed in the paintings at Tassili N'ajjer. After the hunters came cattle herders such as the Fulani in Nigeria. Then came paintings of chariots and horses, almost Cretan

Perhaps one of the good things that have come out of the revolution is that Libyan art, which had been brutally repressed and controlled under Gaddafi, is experiencing a revival.

101

The image of a crocodile engraved into a rock face in Wadi Meggedet. It is estimated to be 12,000 years old.

in style. Lastly, dated to about 100 B.C., there are pictures of people and camels, a clear indication of the changing geography of the Sahara.

AN INSTINCT FOR ORNAMENT

Examining Islamic art, one becomes convinced that Muslim artists hated blank space. But they never made "art for art's sake." Decoration was used to beautify everyday life, so carpets, pottery, windows, fountains, and houses became canvases for Muslim artists.

Libyan craftwork used to include inlaid metalwork, pottery with the glazed tiles called faience, leatherwork, weaving, and embroidery. However, many craft shops have disappeared since Gaddafi encouraged nationalized production. Traditional Berber designs feature zigzags and triangles, often in earthy colors of rusty brown and dark blue. Arab patterns use more flowing, floral shapes known as arabesques.

THEMES

Islamic tradition has favored abstract patterns and elaborate scrollwork, often starkly geometric against a dark background. The polygon is the most common shape. It is easy to see that Muslim artists admired bees with their hexagonal cells for honey, and spiders with star-shaped, concentric webs. Flowers are popular, too, often portrayed as circles or decorated segments.

CARPETS

The origin of the knotted pile rug is lost in time, but certainly the method was invented somewhere in the Middle East, quite possibly in Turkey. It seems likely that these precious and artistic possessions were originally designed as wall hangings rather than rugs to be used underfoot.

The skill of carpet weaving probably came to Libya with the arrival of Islam. And while locally made rugs are still found in Libya, the best ones are imported. The coastal city of Misratah is noted for its carpet industry. Carpet weaving has been called the highest form of art in Islam. Carpets mass-produced in Libya today bear little resemblance to the traditional masterpieces that could take women as long as a year to weave.

The most common form of carpet is the prayer rug, used by Muslims during worship. The arched design imitates the *mihrab* in the mosque that points in the direction of Mecca, which the worshiper must face. A Muslim will unroll a prayer rug in the street or in the desert rather than pray on "unclean" ground.

The interior of a house in the old town of Ghadames. It is decorated with many carpets and rugs.

The design, following Islamic custom, features flowers or geometric patterns. These designs were inspired by a love of gardens and beauty.

MUSIC

The Prophet Muhammad himself seemed to have disapproved of music, fearing perhaps that people might enjoy it too much and forget the seriousness of life. A sanctioned form of music is the chanting of the Koran by a special chanter known for his voice. Koranic chanting is melodious and strikingly beautiful, unaccompanied by musical instruments.

Nevertheless Arab culture finds ways to incorporate music into daily life, and songs and music celebrate special occasions such as feasts and holidays. Arab singers are renowned for their performing abilities and love songs, which are often taken from traditional Bedouin poetry.

Considering its desert origins, it is not surprising to find that Arab music relies on the voice rather than on musical instruments, although the lyre,

Libyan men using handheld drums to accompany their singing during a celebration in Tripoli celebrating the birth of the Prophet Muhammad.

cane pipe, drum, and tambourine accompany the singers' voices. The drum is a major component of Arab music. People like to dance to the music, although men and women are segregated when they dance.

The old poet-singers of the Bedouin sang songs about great deeds or popular heroes, much like the wandering minstrels of medieval Europe. The words were more important than the tune. The *huda* song of the camel drivers has a rhythm that is supposed to echo the movement of the camel's feet.

Music in the Western world is based on a scale of eight notes, with half tones between five of them. Arabic music, on the other hand, has quarter tones as well—a variation that makes tunes sound mournful and exciting, exotic and beautiful.

In addition to traditional musical genres, there is a huge circulation in Libya (as there is everywhere else in the Middle East) of cassettes and CDs of up-to-date North African and foreign popular music, much of which integrates geographically distant instruments and genres.

ARCHITECTURE

An Arab city may seem like a maze of jumbled buildings, but much thought actually goes into its planning. The narrow alleyways provide vital shade, reduce dust, and save space. Privacy is essential—Islamic custom ensures that no door is directly opposite another, and window sills must be at least 5 feet, 9 inches (1.7 m) above ground level. Streets may seem narrow, but they must be wide enough to allow two fully loaded camels to pass each other.

A visitor to Tripoli today will instantly see the contrast between the architect-designed, pastel-shaded villas of the rich suburbs and the shanty towns on the outskirts of the city. Stone-faced minarets rise above domed 18th-century mosques. Beside them are patterned gardens and courtyards. A block away will be the rubble of destroyed hovels or a high-rise apartment building. Traveling south, one sees houses and mosques built of sunbaked mud bricks. Square or with hand-smoothed pointed shapes, they are often whitewashed for a touch of coolness and durability.

CLASSICAL RUINS

Sabratha, 40 miles (64 km) west of Tripoli, holds the remains of a splendid Roman theater that could seat 5,000 people under colonnades 80 feet (24 m)

Libya has a rich history and is home to numerous classical ruins, such as this one at Sabratha.

For the best examples of North African Islamic design, one must look farther west to Kairouan (pictured), once one of the holy cities of Islam in the days when the land was called Ifriqiya. The great mosque there is strictly practical, yet it is one of the most beautiful buildings. A single, huge square minaret acts as a landmark and a fortress gate through which grateful travelers can reach the sheltered enclosure inside (like the yard of the Arab caravanserai—a roadside inn where travelers can rest and recover from the day's journey). The blank outside walls give no hint of the elegant, arcaded courtyard within. The mosque itself has simple round arches that link rows of sturdy columns with just a hint of floral decoration at their tops, giving the impression of an endless forest.

Another example of a classical Greek archaeological site is Cyrene, once the home of famed doctors and the long-vanished medicinal herb, silphium. Julius Caesar had 1,500 pounds (680 kg) of silphium stored away, but by the time Nero became emperor a hundred years later, only one plant could be found in Cyrene for him to use.

After the Arab invasions came the invasion of sand. Many of the marble columns of Leptis Magna were plundered by a French consul as a gift for King Louis XIV to help build the palace of Versailles. Then King George IV acquired what was left of them to make imitation ruins beside Victoria Water, an ornamental lake he had created. The bulk of the cities remained buried until the Italian invasion, when the Italian colonial government, eager to rediscover the greatness of Rome, had them excavated.

And yet the most exciting remains of Libya remain undiscovered. The ruins of Berber and Saharan towns still lie somewhere inland beneath the sweeping sands. They will have to wait, because excavating teams from abroad were not welcomed by the Libyan authorities.

high. At the front of the stage is a marble relief showing the entertainment delights of drama, comedy, dance, and music. The area that was the marketplace had shops with solid stone counters where olives and olive oil, fruit and grain, hides and ivory, and live birds and slaves were sold to Rome.

Even more splendid was Leptis Magna. Once a Carthaginian settlement, it later became a Roman city of 80,000 people. It was brought to its final splendor by one of its own sons, the dark-skinned, black-bearded emperor Septimius Severus. The magnificent public baths were erected under Emperor Hadrian.

Then there are the ruins of Cyrene, situated on a Cyrenaica hillside overlooking the sea. Although they are Greek in origin, the remains are far more Roman, including a forum, a theater, and baths.

BERBER

The Berber culture, which was brutally suppressed under Gaddafi, is now experiencing a revival. Today the town of Jadu has become the center for the rebirth of Amazigh culture and language. Shops have painted Amazigh signs above their doors.

Since the start of the uprising a radio station has been broadcasting from Jadu in both Arabic and Amazigh, in what Berber activists believe are the first conversations in their language over Libyan airwaves in four decades. So far, an Amazigh publishing house has printed four books, billed as Libya's first publications in the language since Gadaffi first seized power.

The Amazigh fear that their culture may be once again undermined, as when the interim Libyan cabinet was unveiled, they found that they were, once again, left unrepresented.

INTERNET LINKS

http://looklex.com/libya/acacus04.htm
This site contains lovely pictures of the rock art of the Acasus Mountains.

LEISURE

A group of men playing a card game in the city of Tripoli.

11

FOR MANY LIBYANS, ESPECIALLY those living in the open desert, leisure is constrained by the need to survive. In pastoral families, when children are old enough, they are expected to help with the household chores and with the herd or crops. Such serious demands leave little time for play.

LEISURE ATTRACTIONS

Libyans living in the cities have no clubs or bars in which to relax. After the revolution Gaddafi shut down night entertainment spots, which encouraged a lifestyle that contradicted strict Islamic law.

Nevertheless there are avenues for recreation in Libya. People in the cities can watch a movie in a theater or meet friends at a café. Sports, especially soccer, are not only leisure pursuits but have become careers for professional athletes. Horse and camel racing are also popular in the country.

Libya has many museums, most of which exhibit archaeological and Islamic artifacts. Examples are the Jamahiriya Museum of Archaeology and Prehistory in the Tripoli Castle, and the Leptis Magna Museum at Al Khums, east of Tripoli.

Libyans enjoy meeting with their friends over cups of tea or at a café. Libyans also like to play card and board games. They enjoy spectator sports such as soccer and horse racing. Hopefully with the end of the civil war, Libyans may once again take to the activities that they love.

The Libyan national soccer team celebrating after their win over Mozambique in the 2012 African World Cup qualifiers.

SPORTS

In the first years of independence, Libya hoped to show its sporting prowess in the international arena. Its Olympic debut was in 1968, when three competitors were sent to the Summer Games in Mexico City. They did not win any medals. After Gaddafi's coup in 1969, there was a very different attitude toward international relations.

At the Munich Olympics in 1972, Palestinian terrorists held several members of the Israeli team hostage and murdered 11 of them. Libya appeared to have been involved. The weapons used by the terrorists had been smuggled into Germany in Libyan diplomatic baggage. When Gaddafi hailed the five terrorists who were killed in the incident as martyr heroes, Libya was banned from participating in the Olympic Games. However, after UN sanctions were suspended in 1999, Libya took part in the Summer Games of 2000 and the Winter Games of 2002. Libya also has a team that participates in the international Special Olympic Games.

Libya's most popular sport is soccer. Matches between local teams are enthusiastically supported, and crowds often gather around a radio to listen to a broadcast. The Libyan Arab Jamahiriya Football Federation, founded in 1962, is a member of international soccer organizations.

HORSES

Horses have been a source of national pride since long before the Arabs arrived in North Africa. In 1229 B.C. an Egyptian pharaoh's soldiers captured 14 chariots from a Libyan chief, which means that horses were being used in Libya over 3,000 years ago. We know that horse-drawn chariots were racing across the Sahara by 1000 B.C. According to the Bedouin, the queen of Sheba gave magnificent Arab stallions to King Solomon. Such horses could easily have come to her kingdom from Africa, through the regular trade route across the Red Sea.

It was the ancestors of the Libyans who introduced the Greeks to four-horse chariot racing. That was also how the Romans caught on to the idea. The Greek historian Herodotus described, in about 470 B.C., how the Garamantes, warriors from Fezzan, chased Ethiopian cave dwellers in their four-horse chariots. The Roman emperor Septimius Severus, from Libya's Leptis Magna, took Arab stallions to Britain as racehorses.

Libyans are mad about horses. There are frequently official and unofficial horse races. And the racing camel, the *mehari* (meh-HAH-ree), is also a mean contender.

The Arabian horse is recognized as the oldest breed in the world. However, it is not certain whether it originated in Arabia as its name suggests. After the Prophet Muhammad was defeated in a battle in A.D. 625 because of a lack of horses, he encouraged horse breeding as a pious and religious duty.

A Libyan man rides a horse at the Benghazi Horse Club.

The Bedouin sing about the speed, loyalty, and beauty of Arabian horses in praise poetry. Here is a translated Bedouin praise poem:

When Allah willed
to create the horse,
He said to the South Wind,
"Of thy substance
shall I create a new being,
for the glory of my chosen people
and the shame of my enemies."
And the South Wind replied,
"Do thou so, Most Mighty."
Then Allah took to himself
a handful of wind,
and breathed upon it
and created a horse
of red-bay color like gold,
and he said, "I name thee horse."

To make sure that horses remained of totally pure pedigree, a horse's ancestry was considered sacred. If horses were captured during the constant raiding, the Arabs promptly set about checking on the pedigree of any captured mare. A messenger would be sent to the defeated side to determine this information. And the information would be given, even if there was a storm of protest at the theft of so wondrous a horse.

Purebred horses were so important that in later years, Muslims were forbidden from selling Arabian horses to Christians so that the stock would remain a unique cultural treasure. Today pure Arabian horses are some of the most distinguished breeds in the world and often win prizes at international competitions.

SCOUTS AND GIRL GUIDES

Scouting activities have spread fast in Libya since their introduction in 1954, even though Gaddafi at one point accused the Boy Scouts of America of being a front for the Central Intelligence Agency. Scouts and Guides in Libya are particularly active in the field of environmental conservation, tree-planting, and building farm roads. They also help the elderly and the handicapped, visit hospitals, and undergo first-aid training. They provide more service to their own community than do Scouts and Guides in some other parts of the world.

And, of course, they go camping. There are national Jamborees every few years, and they take part in joint activities with Scouts and Guides from other African countries. Libyan Scouts and Guides may also go to their meetings in the desert riding camels.

The Libyan Scout's "promise and law" are much the same as for other Scouting associations worldwide. Their motto is *Wa A'eddou* ("Be Prepared").

Now, with the collapse of all government services in Benghazi, the 3,500 Boy Scouts of the city, most between the ages of 8 and 18 years, have been cleaning the streets, distributing food and medicine, assisting doctors and orderlies in hospitals, finding homes for refugees, providing first aid to the injured, giving blood, picking vegetables, unloading aid shipments, clearing shrapnel from the airport runway, making meals for the fighters, and even cleaning the rebels' weapons. "The scouts have been brilliant. We're very proud of them. We underestimated our youth," said Iman Bugaighis, spokeswoman for the Transitional National Council.

TRADITIONAL GAMES

The Bedouin play a game that uses an eight-by-six grid of small holes in the sand. Players in turn place a pebble or bean into a hole and try to get three in a straight line. Each time a player succeeds, he or she removes one of the

The Libyan horse is one of the few natural breeds of the world, which were descended from the original wild horses of central Asia. Among the descendants of the original wild horses of Central Asia are the Spanish horse and the Arabian horse. Libyan horses are mentioned by the Greek historians Herodotus and Xenophon in their writings.

Bedouin men playing a traditional game by digging holes in the sand.

opponent's pebbles. There is also the game of *isseren* (IS-ser-en), which is played by throwing six split sticks into the air and scored by counting how many fall with the split side up. Chess and dominoes are also played.

TOURISM AND TRAVEL

During the 1990s tourism in Libya was nearly nonexistent because of sanctions that prohibited civilian air travel to and from Libya. Since UN sanctions were suspended in 1999, tourism in Libya has become a growing industry, with 149,000 tourists visiting Libya in 2004. This went up to 180,000 tourists in 2007 (this contributed to less than 1 percent of the country's GDP); there were a million day visitors in the same year. Well-preserved Roman ruins at Leptis Magna and the ancient Greek city of Cyrene attracted visitors from all over the world. However, visits to Libya could only be made as part of an organized tour.

Under sanctions, Malta and other countries in the Arab world signed treaties of cooperation with Libya and allowed citizens to enter and travel freely in both countries. Overland trips to neighboring Tunisia and Egypt by bus, and to Malta by boat, were very popular.

After 1999 the number of Libyans traveling abroad increased dramatically, and before the war, they could travel everywhere. Popular vacation destinations included Egypt, Tunisia, Saudi Arabia, Syria, and Malaysia. Few Libyans traveled to Western countries, either because they could not afford it or because they did not feel welcome.

Of course, with the civil war, all tourism to Libya ground to a halt. Most countries issued travel advisories against traveling to Libya as the whole country was a war zone. WIth the end of the civil war, some nations have begun lifting their travel advisories.

Many Libyans have fled Libya as refugees because of the civil war. Most of the foreigners have been evacuated. However stability is gradually being restored and it is hoped that Libyans will be able to return to their country and restore it.

INTERNET LINKS

www.bbc.co.uk/news/world-africa-15700513
Take a look into the UNESCO site, Leptis Magna.

www.ehow.com/list_6716937_traditional-african-children_s-games.html
This enchanting page contains information on traditional African children's games.

www.petcaregt.com/horsecare/horsebreeds/libyanbarbhorse.html
A quick look at the Libya Barb horse.

FESTIVALS

A Tuareg girl in traditional dress for celebrations during the
International Ghat Festival.

12

L IBYA HAS TWO KINDS OF NATIONAL holidays: political and religious. Although the political celebrations take place on fixed days of the year as in the Western world, the religious festivals are part of the Islamic lunar calendar, which means they occur 10 to 12 days earlier every year.

Revolution Day, held on September 1 every year to celebrate Gaddafi's revolution, is understandably not going to be celebrated in Libya any longer.

NATIONAL HOLIDAYS

National Day, the anniversary of the revolution, is on September 1 and is marked with speeches and parades to celebrate the start of the Jamahiriya regime. The other main national holiday is Independence Day on December 24. It celebrates the original granting of independence to the country in 1951.

Libya also celebrates national holidays on March 2 (Declaration of People's Authority), June 11 (Evacuation Day), and October 7 (Italian Evacuation Day).

On Evacuation Day on June 11, Libyans not only celebrate the day when U.S. forces left in 1970, but also commemorate the U.S. bombing of Tripoli by tying black scarves around their heads.

LUNAR CALENDAR

Just like many other Islamic countries in North Africa and the Middle East, Libya follows the Islamic calendar. This means that Islamic years

RAMADAN The month of fasting is signaled by the sighting of the new moon. All healthy adults are expected to fast through the month of Ramadan. Fasting requires Muslims to abstain from food, drink, smoking, and sex between sunrise and sunset.

Visitors to Libya during Ramadan will find themselves forced to observe the fast, whether they are Muslim or not. If they do fast all day, what they will need most at sundown is water. That is why the first meal after nightfall is often a thick,

Libyans in the port city of Benghazi performing late afternoon prayers during Ramadan.

spicy soup, fruit juice, and dates.

Depending on how rich a Libyan family is, there may be more food to follow. As the family eats, they will talk and laugh and play music. In fact, nights can get rowdy. Café nightlife can go on into the early hours of the morning. Ramadan is a time of joy as well as tribulation.

It is during Ramadan that Lailat al-Qadr (LAY-lat ul-KAHD-er), or the Night of Power, is celebrated with readings from the Koran and special prayers. The mosque is full of worshipers on this day. It commemorates the occasion when the angel Gabriel revealed the Koran to the Prophet Muhammad for the first time.

As the month of Ramadan draws to a close, Muslims gather to watch for the new moon. When that appears, there is great rejoicing, for the festival of Id al-Fitr (Id ul-FIT-r) can begin.

ID AL-FITR After a month of fasting, this day of festivity is greeted with joy. The beginning of the day is greeted with the phrase *Id Mubarak*, meaning "happy feast." It is a time for a bath and new clothes, as a reminder that this should be a new beginning in peace and forgiveness. The house is specially decorated. Cards and presents are exchanged and money is given to the poor. Spicy pastries called *samosas* (sah-MOH-sahs) are usually served, along with a variety of sweet cakes and cookies filled with nuts, cream, and dates.

ID AL ADHA The Feast of Sacrifice, or Id al-Adha (Id ul-a-DAH), is the climax of the hajj to Mecca. It commemorates the day when God stopped Abraham, called Ibrahim in the Islamic tradition, from sacrificing his son in obedience to God. Although the festival is mainly for those who have made the pilgrimage to Mecca, it is greeted with four days of rejoicing by all Muslims all over the world.

In memory of the sacrifice, it is customary for Muslim families to sacrifice a sheep on the morning of the feast day and distribute the meat to the poor. This is the time for the whole family to be together. Guests are usually invited to dinner, and greetings are sent to family and friends.

INTERNET LINKS

http://journals.worldnomads.com/worldfestivals/story/32646/Libya/October-Ghadames-Date-Festival-Libya

This website includes a lovely write-up about the Date Festival, complete with a three-minute video.

http://travel.mapsofworld.com/libya/tourism-festivals.html

This site provides information about festivals organized for tourists before the civil war broke out.

www.temehu.com/Calendar.htm

This site includes a description of all the festivals in Libya, complete with a video of the Ghat Festival.

FOOD

A Tuareg man preparing *taajeelah*, bread that is cooked in embers beneath the sand.

13

LIBYA IS ONE OF THE WEALTHIEST countries in Africa, but its population is growing far faster than its food supply. The diet of the average Libyan is unbalanced and lacks protein and essential vitamins.

Libya is a major food importer and the war has disrupted its food supplies. Even though the war has ended, food exporters are reluctant to trade with Libya as they are concerned that the country will not be able to pay them.

Libyan cuisine derives much from the culinary traditions of the Mediterranean and North Africa, with an Italian influence, a legacy from the days when Libya was an Italian colony.

Stall vendors selling fresh produce in a market in Benghazi.

FOOD SUPPLY

Libyans eat large quantities of bread and pasta, usually with a hot peppery sauce, but little meat, fresh fruit, or eggs. In the coastal regions along the Mediterranean, fruit, vegetables, wheat, and barley are grown, but these have to be supplemented by imported foods.

Libya's waters are rich with tuna, sardines, and other fish, but most of the fishing is done by Maltese, Greeks, and Italians. The local catch is not enough to meet the domestic demand, so thousands of tons of fish have to be imported every year.

One of Gaddafi's early policies discouraged small traders and replaced them with large supermarkets run by the state. The quaint Arab market, or souk, with its coffee shops and spice sellers alongside craft and leather stalls, rapidly disappeared. This policy has been changed and local produce is being encouraged once more.

FORBIDDEN FOODS

A store selling dried food and spices.

Muslims all over the world have strict laws about what they may eat and drink. Alcohol is forbidden, as is pork or any food cooked in pork fat. Animals must be killed in a certain way in order for the meat to be considered *halal*, or allowed. The butcher must say a prayer three times before he kills the animal and must kill it in as humane a way as possible.

BEDOUIN MANNERS

A visitor will be served ground coffee or mint tea, followed perhaps by a plate of dates, before any serious conversation starts. Many families in Libya still

RAMADAN NIGHTS

Even though it is spent fasting, the month of Ramadan is a month of special food and drink enjoyed after sundown. Iftar (if-TAAr), or the breaking of the fast, is a very important time for the family to be together. Usually the women of the household spend all day cooking for the evening meal. Dates, a hot lentil soup, and tamarind juice traditionally begin the meal, but after a brief wait, larger and more substantial dishes follow.

Salads and dips of lentils and beans, sizzling grilled meats, spicy rice or couscous, and plenty of hot, flat bread are an essential part of a late-night Ramadan meal. Food is often cooked in abundance so that there is plenty for guests, family, and friends. Desserts and pastries are of special importance during the holy month, when friends and relatives stop by. It would be unthinkable not to have a plate of pastries to offer visitors along with the obligatory tea and coffee. Popular pastries include baklava (bak-LΛ-va), a pistachio and honey pastry with crunchy layers; basbousa (bas-BOO-sa), a semolina cake soaked in flavored syrup; and konafa bil ishta (ko-NAA-fa bill ish-ta), a layered pastry filled with a sweet cream center. Although the pastries can be made at home, the more popular option is to buy huge plates from the local confectioner and bring them home in parcels tied with ribbon.

During the month of Ramadan, Libyans wake up before dawn to have the last meal before sunrise, called suhur (su-HUUR). To wake people, a musician often walks through the neighborhood streets banging a small drum. Suhur is not obligatory for fasting Muslims, but it is a popular option for people who find that they work better on a full stomach. The meal is often a light fruit juice, some rice or pudding, or salad and bread. Because it is at least an hour before sunrise, most people go back to sleep until morning, so the food must be light and easy to digest. Ramadan is a month of different schedules and routines, but a time of joy and togetherness.

eat in the traditional manner. The men usually eat first, while the women wait out of sight once they have served the food. The dishes are placed in the center, with the guests sitting around. No cutlery is used. Only the right hand is used. To use the left hand is considered impure, since the left hand is traditionally used for cleaning up in the bathroom.

To welcome a guest with a proper feast is a delight for the desert Bedouin. Hospitality is a strong part of Islamic custom. Even when times are difficult, a family will prepare special dishes for the guest and make sure that there is plenty of meat—an expensive commodity in Libya. The show of hospitality is a reflection on the status of the family as much as on the guests themselves.

EATING CUSTOMS

At home Libyans eat their meals in a way that originates in Islamic custom. Before and after a meal, they say prayers. Perfumed water may be passed around. In silence each person dips three fingers into the bowl for a ceremonial cleansing.

Before the food is served, a round of bread is placed on each plate. Food is eaten with the fingers. It is the custom for the guest to start eating first; otherwise the eldest in the family will begin. It is not common for Libyans to talk much at meal times.

A baker removing freshly baked bread from the oven.

SPICES

Spices and herbs are essential to Arab cooking. The most common include salt, pepper, saffron, ginger, garlic, cinnamon, cumin, and coriander.

Salt is found in the Sahara Desert in deposits left by long-vanished seas. It is used as a flavoring agent, a preservative, and an antiseptic. Pepper, ground from the dried berries of the pepper vine, gives food a hot, sharp taste.

Saffron, the dried stigmas of a purple-flowered crocus, is used to flavor and color rice. It is the most expensive spice in the world. Ginger is a root that is usually dried and preserved in syrup. It gives a rich tang to meat and fruit. Garlic is a strong-smelling, medicinal herb of the onion family and is used to tenderize meat and flavor salads.

Cinnamon, a fragrant stick of bark, is ground and used as an ingredient in curry powder or in cakes and puddings. Cumin is a sharp-tasting, mildly hot seed that is used whole or powdered in curry. Coriander adds flavor and aroma to many dishes. The seed is used whole or powdered, and the leaves are added to chutneys and sauces.

Bazin, a dish of unleavened dough that is eaten with fish.

After the meal the hands are washed with warm water, and a prayer of thanks is said.

BREAD AND MEAT

Only foreigners in Libya eat leavened bread made with yeast. Most Libyans eat Arab breads such as *kesrah* (KES-raw), a flat pancake made of plain flour without yeast.

Considering that Libyan herdsmen tend about 6 million sheep, it is hardly surprising that lamb is the most common meat. It can be grilled, baked, stewed with vegetables and dates, minced or used in meatballs, and cooked on skewers as kebabs. Spit-roasted baby lamb is a traditional feast among the Bedouin. One popular local dish is a thick soup made with lamb stock and contains vegetables, grains, spices, and small pieces of lamb.

Other popular dishes are *shakshouka* (shak-SHOOK-ah), chopped lamb in tomato sauce with an egg on top; *baba ghanouj* (bah-bah-ga-NOOJ), sesame seeds and eggplant made into a paste, and usually eaten with bread; and *moloukhiya* (moo-LOH-kee-ah), which is steamed vegetables with rice.

DRINKS

In a hot climate, liquid refreshment is essential. Although Libyans grow grapes, their religion forbids the drinking of wine. There are plenty of imported bottled drinks, variations on colas, and fizzy fruit juices. There is also a locally made bright-red sparkling drink called *bitter* (BIT-r) and several hot drinks prepared from ginger, cinnamon, or aniseed.

More popular are coffee and mint tea. Arabs tend to drink their coffee in small cups—thick, black, and very sweet. Mint tea is also found all over Libya as a refreshing hot (and sometimes cold) drink. Libyans are believed to drink more tea per person than people in any other country. The humblest Bedouin tent will have its copper pot brewing over coals, and hospitality demands that a visitor accept at least three glasses or cups of the fragrant, sweetened liquid.

Making tea is a time-honored ritual. The host throws a portion of green tea into a metal teapot and pours boiling water from a kettle, which may sit on its own little brazier. Sugar is added generously, followed by a bouquet of fresh mint. The lid of the teapot is closed, and conversation resumes. After the host has poured tea into his own glass, tasted and tested it, it may at last be offered to his guests and family.

INTERNET LINKS

www.food.com/recipes/libyan

This site contains traditional Libyan recipes with lovely pictures.

www.libyana.org/food/main.htm

This website contains traditional recipes with pictures.

www.temehu.com/Libyan-food.htm

This yummy page includes pictures and descriptions of traditional Libyan food.

LAMB STEW WITH COUSCOUS

Couscous is a staple food in North Africa. It is made from semolina grains and looks like rice. It is usually served with a topping of stew consisting of meat (usually lamb or mutton), vegetables, and chickpeas. This recipe serves four.

2 pounds (1 kg) stewing lamb, cubed

2 onions, chopped

2 cups (500 ml) water

Salt and pepper

1 teaspoon (5 ml) paprika

1 bunch parsley or coriander, fresh chopped

1 teaspoon (5 ml) ground ginger

8 ounces (250 g) each of raisins and pitted prunes, soaked overnight

16 ounces (500 g) precooked couscous

3—4 tablespoons (45—60 ml) olive oil

Put the cubed lamb, one chopped onion, and enough water to cover the meat in a large pot. Add salt and pepper to taste. Add the paprika, parsley or coriander, and ginger. Bring to a boil and cover. Lower heat and simmer for an hour. Add the other onion, and simmer for another 15 minutes. Add the raisins and prunes, and cook for another 10 minutes. Put the couscous in a bowl, and add water a little at a time. Using your fingers, rub the couscous to make sure the grains do not stick together. The couscous should be slightly soft but not lumpy. Mix in the olive oil. Put the couscous in a mesh sieve, and place it directly over the simmering stew, so that the steam rises and warms the couscous. Stir the couscous in the sieve until it is hot and fluffy. Serve hot with the stew.

BASBOUSA WITH ALMONDS

Basbousa, a sweet cake made with semolina and almonds, is a popular dessert in the Middle East. Yogurt is sometimes added to the mix, and cream is spread on top of the basbousa just before serving. This recipe serves four.

3 cups (750 ml) water

2 cups (500 ml) sugar

1 teaspoon (5 ml) lemon juice

1 cup (250 ml) whole almonds, blanched

⅔ cup (170 ml) butter

1 cup (250 ml) semolina

Whole almonds

In a large pot, boil the water, sugar, and lemon juice for a few minutes, stirring the mixture constantly until it becomes thick and syrupy. Remove the mixture from the heat. Chop the almonds into small pieces. In a pan, fry the almonds with the butter and semolina, stirring constantly until dark golden in color. Add the syrup, and cook over low heat for 5 minutes, or until the mixture resembles cookie dough. Take the pan off the stove. Cover and leave to cool for about 5 minutes. Butter an 8-by-8-inch (20-by-20-cm) cake tin, and pour in the slightly cooled mixture about 1 inch (2.5 cm) high. Using a buttered spatula, flatten the mixture. Cut into small squares, and put one blanched almond in the center of each piece. Cool completely and serve.

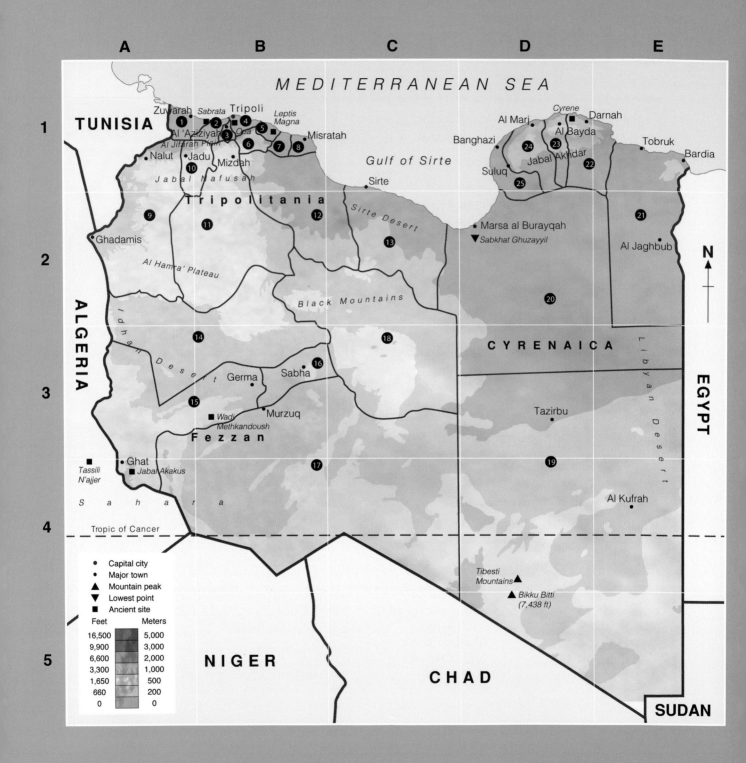

MAP OF LIBYA

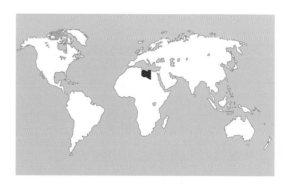

133

ECONOMIC LIBYA

Agriculture

- Barley
- Cattle
- Citrus fruit
- Dates
- Olives
- Peanuts
- Soybeans
- Wheat

Services

- Airport
- Port

Natural Resources

- Natural gas
- Oil

Development Project

- Great Man-Made River

Manufacturing

- Dairy products
- Food processing
- Furniture
- Oil refining
- Textiles
- Water bottling

ABOUT THE ECONOMY

OVERVIEW

Since the outbreak of the civil war, the Libyan economy has ground to a halt. Petroleum production has dropped to zero, alarming many Western economies dependent on Libya's light, sweet crude oil. Before the war, Libya was the world's 12th-largest exporter of crude oil, and was Africa's fourth-largest oil producer after Nigeria, Algeria, and Angola. It produced up to 1.8 million barrels per day and holds estimated reserves of 42 billion barrels. Before the revolution, oil revenues and a small population gave Libya the highest nominal per capita GDP in Africa. Since 2000 Libya had recorded favorable growth rates, with an estimated 10.6 percent growth of GDP in 2010.

GROSS DOMESTIC PRODUCT (GDP)

$90.57 billion (2010 estimate)

GDP PER CAPITA

$14,000 (2010 estimate)

GDP SECTORS

Agriculture, 2.6 percent; industry, 63.8 percent; services, 33.6 percent

CURRENCY

USD 1 = LYD 1.24 (January 2012)
1 Libyan dinar (LYD) = 1,000 dirhams

ECONOMIC GROWTH RATE

4.2 percent (2010 estimate)

LABOR FORCE

1.729 million (2010 estimate)
Services: 59 percent; Industry: 23 percent; Agriculture: 18 percent

UNEMPLOYMENT RATE

32 percent (2010)

IMPORTS

Machinery, semi-finished goods, food, transportation equipment, consumer products

EXPORTS

Crude oil, refined petroleum products, natural gas, chemicals

MAIN TRADE PARTNERS

Italy, Germany, Turkey, France, Tunisia, South Korea, Egypt, United States, China, Spain

OIL RESERVES

46.4 billion barrels (2011)

OIL PRODUCTION

1.8 million barrels/day (2010)

INDUSTRIES

Petroleum, petrochemicals, aluminum, iron and steel, food processing, textiles, handicrafts, cement

AGRICULTURAL PRODUCTS

Wheat, barley, olives, dates, citrus fruit, vegetables, peanuts, soybeans, beef

CULTURAL LIBYA

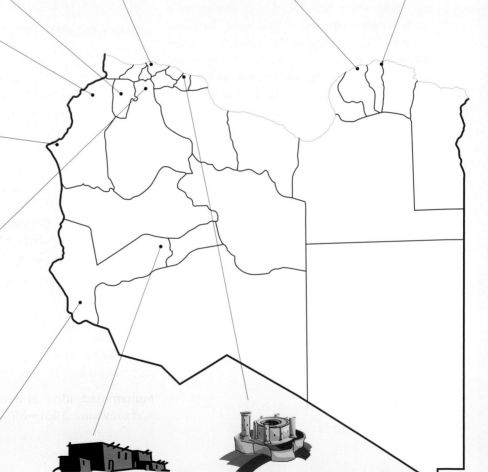

Berber hilltop village
A former desert fortress, Jadu is still an active town and a center of Berber culture, where market days and traditional festivals are a bustle of colorful activity.

Tripoli
Highlights include the old walled city (Medina), the Jamahiriya Museum with artifacts from Roman times, the arch in honor of Roman emperor Marcus Aurelius, souks, and the Red Castle (Assai al-Hamra).

Talmitha
Also known as Ptolemais, this coastal city was a Greco-Roman trading port and storage place for products on their way across the Mediterranean Sea. The ruins excavated here include palaces, fountains, and Roman baths and statues.

Greek ruins
Cyrene, an ancient Greek colony founded in 631 B.C. that later came under Roman rule, has the fountain and sanctuary of Apollo, a forum, a theater, baths, and a large second-century house.

Nalut
This town is famous for its Islamic architecture. The arches and passageways of the old bazaar and the central mosque, both more than 300 years old, are well preserved.

Ghadames
This oasis city, known as the pearl of the desert, is characterized by traditional desert architecture designed to provide cool relief from the desert heat.

Troglodyte dwellings
Until the last decade, the inhabitants of Gharyan lived in caves dug into the mountainside. These cave dwellings are still intact although the dwellers have moved to more modern housing.

Ancient rock art
The Akakus Mountains are home to prehistoric rock art that goes back 10,000 years, stunning rock formations, and caves. Among the rock carvings are those of giraffes, elephants, rhinoceroses, and crocodiles.

Garamantian Civilization
Many tombs, forts, water tunnels, and mud-brick buildings can be found at the site of the Garamantian Empire in Germa and Zinchecra, supposedly inhabited by a warlike people who were skilled chariot riders.

Leptis Magna
Widely regarded as the finest Roman ruins in North Africa, the monuments here include a piazza, elaborate arches, a circus, an amphitheater, a basilica, and the famous Hadrianic baths.

ABOUT THE CULTURE

OFFICIAL NAME
Great Socialist People's Libyan Arab Jamahiriya

NATIONAL FLAG
A cresent moon and star on a triband (red, black, and green) background. This flag was first used when Libya gained independence in 1951. It replaced Gaddafi's all-green flag after he was deposed.

NATIONAL SYMBOL
A black-and-gold eagle with a shield on its breast

POPULATION
6.6 million (July 2011)

POPULATION GROWTH RATE
2.064 percent (2011)

LITERACY
82.6 percent (2011)

CAPITAL
Tripoli

OTHER MAJOR CITIES
Benghazi, Tobruk, Sirte, Musratah, Zuwarah, Darnah, Sabha, Ghadames

GOVERNMENT
Constitutional democracy

OFFICIAL LANGUAGE
Arabic (official); English and Italian are also spoken

LIFE EXPECTANCY
75.34 years for men, 80.08 years for women

GEOGRAPHICAL REGIONS
Tripolitania, Cyrenaica, Fezzan

RELIGION
Islam

ADMINISTRATIVE REGIONS
Al Butnan, Darnah, Al Jabal al Akhdar, Al Mari, Benghazi, Al Wahat, Al Kufrah, Sirt, Murzuq, Sabha, Wadi Al Hayaa, Misrata, Al Murgub, Tarabulus, Al Jfara, Az Zawiyah, An Nuqat al Khams, Al Jabal al Gharbi, Nalut, Ghat, Al Jufrah, Wadi Al Shatii

ETHNIC GROUPS
Berber and Arab, 97 percent; other, 3 percent (includes Greeks, Maltese, Italians, Egyptians, Pakistanis, Turks, Indians, and Tunisians)

LEADERS IN POLITICS
Muhammad Idris al-Sanusi—Libya's first and only king (1951—69)
Muammar Gaddafi—chairman of the Revolutionary Command Council and head of state (1969—2011)
Mustafa Abdel Jalil—chairman of the National Transitional Council (March 23, 2011)

TIME LINE

IN LIBYA	IN THE WORLD
A.D. 642	
Umayyad general Amr Ibn Al-As conquers the Libyan coast for the Islamic empire.	1206–1368
909	Genghis Khan unifies the Mongols and starts conquest of the world. At its height, the Mongol Empire under Kublai Khan stretches from China to Persia and parts of Europe and Russia.
Libya falls to the Fatimad dynasty.	
1510	
Spanish forces capture Tripoli.	
1551	
Ottoman armies reclaim Libya.	1776
	U.S. Declaration of Independence
	1789–99
1911	The French Revolution
The Italians land in Tripoli.	1914
	World War I begins.
	1939
1940	World War II begins.
Fighting during World War II begins in the deserts of Libya and Egypt.	1945
1951	The United States drops atomic bombs on Hiroshima and Nagasaki. World War II ends.
The United Nations declares Libya an independent country. Muhammad Idris al-Sanusi becomes the first king.	
1969	
The September Revolution brings Colonel Muammar Gaddafi into power.	
1980	
Gaddafi announces the annexation of the Tibesti Mountains in Chad. French troops intervene and a long war begins.	
1989	
Libya signs a peace treaty with Chad and withdraws from the Tibesti Mountains.	
1992	
The United Nations imposes sanctions on Libya for harboring the Lockerbie suspects.	1997
1999	Hong Kong is returned to China.
Libya agrees to hand over the Lockerbie suspects. The United Nations suspends the sanctions, but the U.S. trade embargo remains.	

IN LIBYA	IN THE WORLD
2001 The Lockerbie trial ends. Diplomatic relations with Western governments improve.	**2001** Terrorists crash planes into New York, Washington D.C., and Pennsylvania.
2003 The United Nations lifts sanctions on Libya.	**2003** War in Iraq begins.
	2004 Eleven Asia countries are hit by giant tsunami, killing at least 225,000 people.
2005 Libya's first auction of oil and gas exploration licenses heralds the return of U.S. energy companies for the first time in more than 20 years.	**2005** Hurricane Katrina devastates the Gulf Coast of the United States.
2008 Libya takes over a one-month rotating presidency of the UN Security Council. Italian Prime Minister Silvio Berlusconi apologizes to Libya for the damage inflicted by Italy during the colonial era and signs a $5 billion investment deal by way of compensation. U.S. Secretary of State Condoleezza Rice makes a historic visit—the highest-level U.S. dignitary visit to Libya since 1953.	**2008** Earthquake in Sichuan, China, kills 67,000 people.
2009 Gaddafi is elected chairman of the African Union by leaders meeting in Ethiopia.	**2009** Outbreak of flu virus H1N1 around the world
2010 Russia agrees to sell Libya weapons in a deal worth $1.8 billion.	
2011 Bloody Libyan civil war lasts eight months from February to October, when Gaddafi is captured and killed. An interim government is announced later in the year.	**2011** Twin earthquake and tsunami disasters strike northeast Japan, leaving more than 14,000 dead and thousands more missing.

GLOSSARY

Amazigh
Another term for the Berbers, who are thought to be the indigenous people of North Africa.

***bayt* (bait)**
An extended family unit.

Bedouin
A desert nomad.

Carthage
An ancient civilization in North Africa.

Fezzan
The inland desert of Libya.

***Ghibli* (GIB-lee)**
A sandstorm.

halal
Food that Muslims are allowed to consume.

imam
The religious leader of a mosque.

***Kesrah* (kes-RAW)**
Libyan bread, made without yeast.

Kharijite
One of the sects of Islam.

Leptis Magna
The ruins of an ancient Roman city in Libya located in Al Khums, to the east of Tripoli.

Maghreb
The Berber area of North Africa, normally including Morocco, Algeria, Libya, and Tunisia.

***Mehari* (meh-HAH-ree)**
A pedigreed racing camel.

Oea
An ancient Roman city that occupied Tripoli's present-day location.

Phoenicians
The inhabitants of Phoenicia, an ancient region where present-day Lebanon is located.

Salaam Aleikum
A traditional Arab greeting that means "peace be with you."

sheikh
The head of an Arab village or camp.

souk
A covered market with many small shops.

Tassili N'ajjer
A mountainous area of the Sahara, in Algeria near Libya's southwestern border.

Tuareg
A nomadic desert people related to the Berbers.

wadi
A dry valley that sometimes forms an oasis.

FOR FURTHER INFORMATION

BOOKS

Ham, Anthony. *Lonely Planet Libya: Country Travel Guide Lonely Planet.* London: Lonely Planet Publications, 2011.

John, Sir Ronald Bruce. *Libya: From Colony to Independence* (One World Short Histories). London: One World, 2008.

Kawczynski, Daniel. *Seeking Gaddafi.* Colorado Springs, CO: Dialogue Publishing Inc., 2011.

Matar, Hisham. *In the Country of Men.* New York: Dial Press Trade Paperback, 2008.

Thomas Cook Publishing. *Travelers Libya* (Travelers Thomas Cook). Peterborough, England: Thomas Cook Publishing, 2009.

Vandewalle, Dirk. *A History of Modern Libya.* Cambridge, England: Cambridge University Press, 2006.

Wright, John. *A History of Libya* (Columbia/Hurst). New York: Columbia University Press, 2010.

DVDs

7 Days Libya. TravelVideoStore.com, 2010.

Cosmos Global Documentaries: Tripolitania—Libya. TravelVideoStore.com, 2009.

Global Treasures Leptis Magna Libya. TravelVideoStore.com, 2005.

MUSIC

Arabian Delight: Music from Egypt Libya Tunisia Algeria. Abdu El-Hanid, Smithsonian Folkways, 2010.

Folk Music of the Sahara: Among the Tuareg of Libya. Hisham Mayet, 2004.

WEBSITES

BBC News Country Profiles: Libya. http://news.bbc.co.uk/2/hi/middle_east/country_profiles/819291.stm

CIA World Factbook Libya. https://www.cia.gov/library/publications/the-world-factbook/geos/ly.html

Guardian.co.uk—Libya. www.guardian.co.uk/world/libya

Library of Congress Federal Research Division Country Studies: Libya. http://lcweb2.loc.gov/frd/cs/lytoc.html

Libya News—Topix. www.topix.com/world/libya

Libya On Line Information and Entertainment at your fingertips. www.libyaonline.com

Libyana: Culture of Libya. www.libyana.org

Lonely Planet World Guide: Destination Libya. www.lonelyplanet.com/destinations/africa/libya

New York Times: Libya—Protests and Revolts 2011. http://topics.nytimes.com/top/news/international/countriesandterritories/libya/index.html

The Sabr Foundation Islam 101. www.islam101.com

The Telegraph—Libya News. www.telegraph.co.uk/news/worldnews/africaandindianocean/libya/

UN Security Council Global Policy Forum: Libya. www.globalpolicy.org/security/sanction/libya/indxirlb.htm

BIBLIOGRAPHY

BOOKS

Ham, Anthony. *Lonely Planet Libya: Country Travel Guide Lonely Planet*. London: Lonely Planet Publications, 2011.

John, Sir Ronald Bruce. *Libya: From Colony to Independence* (One World Short Histories). London: One World, 2008.

Kawczynski, Daniel. *Seeking Gaddafi*. Colorado Springs, CO: Dialogue Publishing Inc., 2011.

Matar, Hisham. *In the Country of Men*. New York: Dial Press Trade Paperback, 2008.

Thomas Cook Publishing. *Travelers Libya* (Travelers Thomas Cook). Petersborough, England: Thomas Cook Publishing, 2009.

Vandewalle, Dirk. *A History of Modern Libya*. Cambridge, England: Cambridge University Press, 2006.

Wright, John. *A History of Libya* (Columbia/Hurst). New York: Columbia University Press, 2010.

WEBSITES

Acasus Mountains Rock Art. http://looklex.com/libya/acacus04.htm

Ancient Language Renewed in Libyan Rebellion. http://news.nationalpost.com/2011/07/11/ancient-language-renewed-in-libyan-rebellion/

Anglo-Libyan—Libya's Endangered Wildlife. www.anglo-libyan.com/2006/12/libyas-endangered-animals.html

Food.com—Libyan Recipes. www.food.com/recipes/libyan

Global Edge: Libya—Economy. http://globaledge.msu.edu/countries/libya/economy/

How Is Religion Informing Libyan Rebels?. www.washingtonpost.com/blogs/guest-voices/post/how-is-religion-informing-the-rebels-in-libya/2011/04/02/AF8VXmRC_blog.html

Islam 101. http://islam101.net/

Islam.com. www.islam.com/

Libya Country Profile—Library of Congress. http://lcweb2.loc.gov/frd/cs/profiles/Libya.pdf

Libya Crisis: The Story So Far. www.bbc.co.uk/news/world-africa-13860458

Libya: Increasing Healthcare Needs—International Committee of the Red Cross (ICRC). www.icrc.org/eng/resources/documents/update/2011/libya-update-2011-07-05.htm

Libya's History Sheds Light on Current Conflict. www.npr.org/2011/03/07/134336993/Libyas-History-Sheds-Light-On-Current-Conflict

Libyan Customs. www.ewpnet.com/libya/customs.htm

Libyan English-language Radio Station Carries on in the Face of Attacks. www.guardian.co.uk/world/2011/may/29/libya-english-radio-tribute-fm

Libyana Food. www.libyana.org/food/main.htm

Linguistic Diversity in Libya. http://lughat.blogspot.com/2011/03/linguistic-diversity-in-libya.html

Mongabay.com—Libya Geography. www.mongabay.com/reference/country_studies/libya/GEOGRAPHY.html

Rebel Leadership Casts a Wide Net. http://online.wsj.com/article/SB10001424052748704629104576190720901643258.html

Saving the World Economy from Gaddafi. http://rt.com/news/economy-oil-gold-libya/

Stalemate in Libya between rebels and Gaddafi Loyalists. www.time.com/time/photogallery/0,29307,2053369,00.html

Temehu—Wildlife in the Sahara. www.temehu.com/Wild-life-in-sahara.htm

Temehu.com—Libyan Food. www.temehu.com/Libyan-food.htm

The Libyan Interim National Council. www.ntclibya.org/english/

Travel Document Systems—TDS—Libya. www.traveldocs.com/ly/economy.htm

INDEX

INDEX